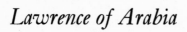

Lawrence of Arabia

LOUISIANA STATE UNIVERSITY PRESS
BATON ROUGE

Lawrence
OF
Arabia

THE LITERARY IMPULSE

Stanley Weintraub & Rodelle Weintraub

ISBN 0–8071–0152–4
Library of Congress Catalog Card Number 74–27195
Copyright © 1975 by Louisiana State University Press
All rights reserved
Manufactured in the United States of America

This book was designed by Dwight Agner and
composed in Monotype Janson by Michael & Winifred Bixler,
Boston, Massachusetts. It was printed and bound by
LithoCrafters, Inc., Ann Arbor, Michigan.

If you keep unstained the honour of your house
  Any rags you wear will look beautiful.
If you fail to overcome yourself
  You will receive no honour from the world.

—T. E. Lawrence's adaptation of
an Arabic poem by King Feisal

To Muz and Dad

Contents

Preface

T. E. LAWRENCE'S highest ambition was literary. Although he could have had flamboyant careers in politics or in the military, in government or in society, in industry, banking, or education, after the Arabian experience he wanted none of them and almost found contentment in the ranks as "Private Shaw" — a name he eventually (and quietly) adopted legally. Still one ambition remained: He desired neither praise from Allenby for his military exploits nor Churchillian offers of government posts for his statecraft; not the Royal Air Force commissions tendered by Air Marshal Trenchard, the secretaryship of the Bank of England offered by Montagu Norman, the honorary doctorates offered by English universities, nor equivalent worldly rewards attracted by "Lawrence of Arabia." He merely wanted to write some of the best prose in the language and to gain recognition for having done so. He wanted to write one of the greatest books of his time, and he may have—but when he had completed his final version of it, he despaired that he had failed.

Lawrence found despair as necessary as ambition. He lived on the masochistic side of asceticism, and the non-physical part of his self-punishment involved creating within himself a sense of deep frustration to immediately follow, and cancel out, high achievement by denying himself the honors he had earned. At its most extreme it involved a symbolic killing of the self, a taking up of a new life and a new name. Still, he could not kill off the literary impulse. He returned to the semimonasticism of the ranks and wrote starkly about the self-punishment of its discipline which—although too old for it—he had chosen to endure; and he agonized over other opportunities to prove himself as a writer as he had proved himself in the life of action. The goad of desire was there; his ability to handle language was already palpable; but inspiration failed him. The manner of his untimely death, at forty-six, only added to the complexities of his myth.

"What could be more extraordinary," Malcolm Muggeridge asked viciously a generation later, "than the survival of his cult, which flourishes the more as his lies and attitudinizing are made manifest? He . . . is superlatively a case of everything being true except the facts. Who more fitting to be a Hero of Our Time than this, our English Genet, or Sodomite Saint, with Lowell Thomas for his Sartre and Alec Guinness to say amen?"

To Kingsley Amis, Lawrence is a "sonorous fake," and a scattering of critics have always expressed similar scepticism; yet his writing survives, and it survives criticism. That Lawrence's work as a writer is worth serious attention is no longer in doubt. As Malcolm Lowry wrote a friend about *Seven Pillars of Wisdom*, "It's wholly marvellous and makes most prose look silly." Lowry had no need to flatter Lawrence (as some of T.E.'s literary friends may have been tempted to do), for by then T.E. had been dead for twenty-eight years. Together with Lawrence's sharply etched service chronicle *The Mint*, *Seven Pillars* was in several ways the precursor for a school of writing which was to become increasingly influential in midcentury. His rendering of the *Odyssey*—not only in his lifetime but, more to the point, after many intervening translations—has been called one of the finest in English. And his immense and fascinating correspondence, increasingly emerging into print, establishes him as one of the major letter-writers of his century.

Our glance at Lawrence the writer follows these aspects of his claim—one he would have been reluctant to make himself—for his place in the literature of his time. Since Lawrence the writer is inextricable from Lawrence the man, his writings are observed in the context of that complex portion of his life in which his ambitions were primarily literary. If elements of the Lawrence "myth" remain, it is in part because myth, when successful, replaces reality—and that in itself is a tribute to Lawrence's power with words. Since a preponderant portion of the Lawrence legend was a self-portrait from life, the most useful pages on Lawrence the man of letters can be written by no one but Lawrence himself. It can be said more truly of Lawrence than of most writers—the man is in his books.

Stanley Weintraub
Rodelle Weintraub

Acknowledgments

THE AUTHORS are grateful for help received over years of work on T. E. Lawrence from his brother A. W. Lawrence. They are also grateful for assistance from others who knew Lawrence as a man and a man of letters, particularly Brian Carter, David Garnett, Robert Graves, H. Jackson, Kenneth Marshall, the late Sir Basil Liddell Hart, and the late F. L. Lucas.

Works of T. E. Lawrence are cited or quoted from sources and editions as acknowledged in the notes. For permission to utilize Lawrence's writings the authors are indebted to Jonathan Cape, Ltd. (both as publisher and as agent for the Lawrence literary estate), Doubleday, and Oxford University Press.

CHAPTER I

Evolution of an Epic: The Early Writings

THE first conjunction of Lawrence with Arabia came in the summer of 1909, when T.E. was twenty and was reading history at Oxford. Interested in medieval fortified castles, he planned his undergraduate thesis around a study of them and, contrary to expert advice, set off in summer, and on foot, on a solitary tour of crusader castles in Turkish-held Syria and Palestine. He acquired some broken bones, malaria, and dysentery; he ate irregularly and was shot at regularly. Near the end of his expedition he was beaten, robbed, and left for dead by a band of Kurds. Still, he had examined and taken notes on thirty-six castles; and back in England he produced an Honours Thesis, taking a first class in history in 1910.

"The thesis was not for publication," T.E. wrote Major Archibald Beck in 1929, "& I have no idea what happened to it; I lent it to Lord Curzon about 1919; and I don't remember it since (Except for a half-notion that he gave it me back & I burned it: but I don't remember this well enough to swear to it. It was only a thesis—a first study. Not worth printing.): a typescript, it was, with plans & photos." As *Crusader Castles*, it was published by the Golden Cockerel Press in two volumes after his death. The first volume contains the thesis submitted to Jesus College, Oxford: "The Influence of the Crusades on European Military Architecture to the End of the 12th Century." The second includes selected letters written by T.E. while on visits to crusader castles in France, England, Wales, and Syria in search of data.

Lawrence's first months after graduation were spent in desultory archeological study in the British Museum and among the antiquities in Oxford's Ashmolean Museum. Toward the end of the year, he was awarded a postgraduate scholarship at Magdalen College and joined an Oxford expedition to Jerablus to help in the excavation of the great Hittite mounds at Carchemish, on the Euphrates. For most of the next three years the dig was to be his headquarters. Between excavations, and learning how to become a reasonable facsimile of the Arab workmen employed on the dig, he went off—dressed in the manner of the country—on solitary walking tours, acquiring scant information and considerable fever and dysentery.

One of the sites to which he was directed in northern Syria led to what was probably his first publication, "The Kaer of Ibu Wardani," which appeared in the first volume of the *Jesus College Magazine*, in January, 1913, under the initials "C.J.G." (At the very start Lawrence was writing under pseudonyms.) Although the Arabs believed the Kaer was built by an Eastern prince as a desert palace for his queen, T.E. reported it was a ruin of the Roman period. Its gaping emptiness emphasized the harshness of the desert to Lawrence, who later adapted the piece to other uses in *Seven Pillars of Wisdom*, where in the chapter "A God of Negations" (III) the ruin emphasizes the forced simplicity of Bedouin life.

Curiously enough, Lawrence's brief return to Syria from Sinai in the spring of 1914 had literary consequences he may never have known. That year Maurice Barrès was in Syria gathering material for his crusader castle story, *Un Jardin sur l'Oronte* (Paris, 1922), on the second page of which he wrote that in June, 1914, "ce jeune savant, un Irlandais, charge par le British Museum des fouilles de Djerablous sur l'Euphrate, un heureuse fortune venait de me le faire recontrer qui flanait comme moi dans les ruelles du bazar." Did an unnamed young Irish archeologist possessed of some Arabic translate the story then and there for Barrès, as he pretends in his preface? Did Lawrence, ever eager to talk about crusader castles, not only tap the reservoir of his own Oxford thesis as well as his travels but describe himself, not erroneously, as an Irishman?* Whatever the actual facts, no one else fits Barrès' description.

In his last prewar expedition Lawrence left Syria to accompany archeologist Leonard Woolley (his last chief at Carchemish) and a Royal Engineers officer, S. F. Newcombe, into the Sinai Peninsula, on the Turkish frontier east of Suez. Supposedly a scientific trip, it served primarily as camouflage for a map-making reconnaissance from Gaza to Aqaba, des-

* Lawrence's father, heir to an Irish baronetcy, left County Meath, his wife, and four daughters to run away with the governess, by whom he had five sons. Only the first son, Robert, was born in Ireland. Thomas Edward, the second, was born in Wales on August 16, 1888. By that time his father had changed his name from Chapman to Lawrence.

tined to be of strategic value even sooner than anticipated, for the year was 1914.

The report of the expedition, *The Wilderness of Zin*, was published under the names of both Woolley and Lawrence in 1915 by the Palestine Exploration Fund. Woolley was a prolific writer on archeological subjects for years; from the text, there is no way to separate the contributions of the collaborators, but parts of it have the ring of the dramatic descriptive prose of Lawrence's letters home and his earlier *Crusader Castles*.

From this plain one comes quite suddenly to the edge of the plateau, the pilgrim way from Suez falls in on the right, and the united roads turn sharply down a little valley that is the beginning of the Nagb or pass of Aqaba.

The way down is very splendid. In the hillsides all sorts of rocks are mingled in confusion; grey-green limestone cliffs run down sheer for hundreds of feet, in tremendous ravines whose faces are a medley of colours wherever crags of black porphyry and diorite jut out, or where soft sandstone, washed down, has left long pink and red smudges on the lighter colours. The confusion of materials makes the road-laying curiously uneven. The surface is in very few cases made up; wherever possible the road was cut to rock, with little labour, since the stone is always brittle and in thin, flat layers. So the masons had at once ready to their hand masses of squared blocks for parapets or retaining walls. Yet this same facility of the stone has been disastrous to the abandoned road, since the rains of a few seasons chisel the softer parts into an irregular giant staircase; while in the limestone the torrent has taken the road-cutting as a convenient course, and left it deep buried under a sliding mass of water-worn pebbles.[1]

Lawrence returned to England the month the war began, and shifted rapidly from his role as a civilian employee of the War Office in London, charged with preparing a militarily useful map of Sinai,* to that of impudent young lieutenant in

---

* With three others, he produced a map "eighteen feet each way in three colours. Some of it was accurate, and the rest I invented."

Cairo, insignificant in stature or job, his duties at first little changed from his civilian ones. Restless and vaguely ambitious, he found his new position an amazing bit of luck. "Experts" on Arab affairs, especially those who had traveled in the Turkish-held Arab lands, were rare, and T.E. was assigned to Intelligence. He spent more than a year based in Egypt, interviewing Turkish prisoners, drawing maps, producing a handbook on the Turkish army, receiving data from agents behind enemy lines—and acting the part of Least Professional Officer in the British army. He dressed with ostentatious sloppiness and otherwise exasperated officialdom by his offhand manner, his exaggerated respect to superiors, and his noisy motorcycle. He went off on minor intelligence missions to Greece and Libya and for a while enjoyed the intrigue and confusion common to all headquarters staffs. But in the middle of 1915 his brothers Frank and Will were killed in action, and T.E. was cruelly reminded of the more active front in the West. Feeling guilty in his security, he considered applying for a transfer to France.

Egypt at the time was the staging area for military operations of prodigious inefficiency—wasteful desert campaigns against the Turks and a bloody, bungled frontal assault on the Dardanelles at Gallipoli. Lawrence's informal suggestions to his superiors were to take advantage of Arab efforts at rebellion by abetting them with smuggled-in arms and money, and to make use of the dissident sheikhs by meshing their aspirations for independence from the Turks to general military strategy. In their predicament, strategy-planners were even willing to listen to the young officer in Cairo who was one of a group then editing and writing a secret intelligence periodical called the *Arab Bulletin*, meant to keep British diplomats and military commands all over the Middle East informed about developments within Arab lands controlled by the Germans and Turks.

Lawrence was not the only officer to become involved in the mission of inciting an Arab uprising, but he quickly became—at least according to his account—its brains, its organizing force, its liaison with Cairo, and its military technician. His small second-front behind Turkish lines was a hit-and-run guerrilla operation, specializing in the mining of bridges and supply trains and the appearance of Arab units first in one place, then another, tying up enemy forces which might have been deployed elsewhere. Lawrence—"Emir Dynamite" to the admiring Bedouins—committed the cynical, self-serving sheikhs for the moment to his kingmaker's vision of a unified Arab nation, goaded them when their spirits flagged with examples of his own self-punishing personal valor, bribed them with promises of enemy booty and new supplies of gold and automatic weapons. By the time the motley Arab army reached Damascus in October, 1918, Lawrence was physically and emotionally exhausted, having too often forced body and spirit to the breaking point. He had been wounded numerous times; been captured, tortured, and homosexually abused; endured endless privations of hunger and weather and disease; been driven by military necessity to commit atrocities upon the enemy and murder his own wounded to prevent the Turks from doing worse; and witnessed in Damascus the defeat of his aspirations for the Arabs in the very moment of their triumph, their factionalism having rendered them incapable of becoming a nation. Anglo-French duplicity, T.E. knew, had already betrayed them in a cynical wartime division of expected spoils. Disillusioned and distinguished, Lawrence left for England just before the armistice and, at a royal audience on October 30, 1918, politely refused the Order of the Bath and the D.S.O., leaving the shocked King George V "holding the box in my hand."[2]

A colonel at thirty, Lawrence was a private at thirty-four. In between he lobbied vainly for Arab independence at the Paris Peace Conference in 1919, even appearing in Arab robes; later in the same year he was the sole survivor of the crash of a Handley-Page bomber at Rome in which he injured his head, broke some ribs and his collarbone, and permanently damaged a lung. Meanwhile, he worked on *Seven Pillars of Wisdom*, his epic-memoir of Arabia, acquiring for the purpose an All Souls College fellowship;* and all the while—beginning in London in August, 1919—he was being transformed into a living legend by Lowell Thomas' long-run illustrated lecture, "With Allenby in Palestine and Lawrence in Arabia" (which T.E. enjoyed going to see). In March, 1921, T.E. was wooed back to the Middle East as Colonial Minister Churchill's adviser, redeeming where he could the idealistic wartime promises he had made. But the poetic ideal had splintered. Rather than an Arab nation, there were groupings of historically hostile tribes. And the Arabian lands had been divided into politically exigent states. One—the Palestine mandate—Lawrence helped split into Palestine and a Transjordanian Hashemite monarchy. (He had long supported the idea of a Jewish "national home" in what is now Israel. It was in the best interests of both Arab and Jew, he insisted, for Jews in Palestine had already begun demonstrating to the

---

* The fellowship actually became effective in November, 1919. Lawrence was in continuous residence in Oxford only briefly and returned intermittently during the seven-year span of the fellowship.

region how the inimical soil could be made to flower and to support a people.) The crazy lines which divided the postwar Middle East for the most part parceled out spheres of European influence and divided feuding Arab factions from one another. Reflecting upon either motive could not have made him happy with what he had helped bring about.

Lawrence had already written voluminous notes on his role and at least two versions of a war memoir based upon them, in which he expounded not only his dream for that troubled part of the world but his tribulations with the Arabs whom he had once loved as brothers. He had written not only of their loyalty, courage, and hardihood but, in disillusion, of their tribal feuds and treachery which often destroyed his carefully laid plans. And he had described, in sorrow, the times when those on whom he had counted most would flee at the first sound of heavy artillery or desert their own cause when not bribed with British gold or promises of booty. Still, he had done what he could, and he bathed his accounts with a romantic nostalgia that sometimes turned the desert tribesmen into knights and princes of a near-medieval epic.

After the Cairo political settlements, Churchill asked Lawrence to remain in the Colonial Ministry, but T.E. wanted no part of high government office and had already chosen a course opposite in the extreme. In August, 1922, under an assumed name, he enlisted in the Royal Air Force. By then he had completed the rough printing—on an Oxford newspaper press—of eight double-columned copies of his memoir—the first, but not the last, printed version of *Seven Pillars of Wisdom*. He had intended using the title for an earlier work he afterwards curiously described as an "imaginary book on C P Cairo Smyrna Aleppo Jerusalem Urfa and Damascus, destroyed by T.E.S. in August 1914."[3] (The biblical title came from the Book of Proverbs [9:1]—"Wisdom hath builded a house: she hath hewn out her seven pillars"—and had little relationship to the subject matter of Lawrence's book-in-progress other than sentimental association with the same part of the world.)*

The original *Seven Pillars* remains a mysterious work, but it was not an ex post facto invention of Lawrence's, meant to feed a myth. "You will see," he had written home in 1911 about a projected private press, "that printing is not a business but a craft. . . . And besides such a scheme would be almost sure to interrupt the *Seven Pillars of Wisdom* or my monumental book on the Crusades." A year later, clearly in response to a query from home about his writing, he explained:

I am not trying to rival Doughty. You remember that passage that he who has once seen palm-trees and the goat-hair tents is never the same as he had been: that I feel very strongly, and I feel also that Doughty's two years wandering in untainted places made him the man he is, more than all his careful preparations before & since. My books would be the better, if I had been for a time in open country: and the Arab life is the only one that still holds the early poetry which is the easiest to read.

* Later T.E. imposed upon the postwar *Seven Pillars of Wisdom* a tentative outline (now in a notebook in the Houghton Library, Harvard University) which extended the architectural metaphor:
  Book I—Materials
  Book II—Survey
  Book III—Foundations
  Book IV—Scaffolding
  Book V—Pillars
  Book VI—Failures
  Book VII—Reconstruction
  Book VIII—The House Is Perfected
The plan was abandoned in the ten-book final version, in which the metaphor nearly disappears, except for such dramatic touches as Feisal's being described as "very tall and pillar-like." The architectural part-titles disappear altogether.

Thus there *was* a book, "a youthful indiscretion book," he called it later. "It recounted adventures in seven type-cities of the East (Cairo, Bagdad, Damascus, etc.) and arranged their characters into a descending cadence: a moral symphony. It was a queer book, upon whose difficulties I look back with a not ungrateful wryness: and in memory of it I so named the new book." He burned the manuscript, he said, the month the war began.

Even early in the war it was obvious that Lawrence had a compulsion to write, although his channels necessarily had to be nonliterary ones. Aside from his *Arab Bulletin* papers he kept a scrappy journal and produced several lengthy political and military essays meant for official eyes. One, "The Politics of Mecca," written in January, 1916, and meant for General Staff Intelligence in Cairo, stressed the instability of the Arabs as a potential nation and suggested shrewdly the value of such an insight to English power in the area. Yet even here he could not resist compelling literary touches. "If properly handled," he predicted of the Arabs, "they would remain in a state of political mosaic, a tissue of small jealous principalities incapable of cohesion."[4] Soon afterwards he wrote a long memorandum entitled "The Conquest of Syria: If Complete," setting out the politics and tactics he proposed for the Arab revolt and which he carefully followed himself—and persuaded the Arabs to follow—as soon as he had the opportunity. Again it was a document with a wit and a wryness unusual in staff papers. Lawrence forecast:

This war should, if it resulted in anything at all, take away definitely and finally the religious supremacy of the Sultan [of Turkey]. England cannot make a new Khalifa [spiritual ruler] as she has made a new Sultan [in occupied Egypt] any more than the Japanese could impose a new Pope on the

R C Church. Nor can the Sultan of Egypt make himself Khalifa: for his action would be suspect, from his relations with us; and the true Arab and even the Syrian has such a lively contempt and dislike for the loose-mouthed Egyptian as would entirely forbid him ever to recognize any spiritual overlordship assumed by one without the force to support him.[5]

Equally wry and candid was his "Twenty-Seven Articles," a manual for political officers on how to manipulate Arabs which T.E. wrote in August, 1917, after nearly a year in the field with Feisal's army. "Handling Hejaz Arabs," he warned in a preface, "is an art, not a science." And Lawrence artfully explained the techniques:

If you can wear Arab kit when with the tribes you will acquire their trust and intimacy to a degree impossible in uniform. It is however danger-ous and difficult. . . . You will be like an actor in a foreign theatre, playing a part day and night for months, without rest, and for an anxious stake. Com-plete success, which is when the Arabs forget your strangeness and speak naturally before you, counting you one of themselves, is perhaps only at-tainable in character; while half success (all that most of us will strive for—the other costs too much) is easier to win in British things, and you yourself will last longer, physically and mentally, in the comfort that they mean. . . . If you wear Arab things wear the best. Clothes are significant among the tribes, and you must wear the appropriate, and appear at ease in them. Dress like a Sherif—if they agree to it.

. . . .

If you wear Arab things at all, go the whole way. Leave your English friends and customs on the coast, and fall back on Arab habits entirely. It is possible, starting thus level with them, for the European to beat the Arabs at their own game, for we have stronger motives for our action, and put more heart into it then they. If you can surpass them, you have taken an immense stride towards complete success, but the strain of living and thinking in a foreign and half-understood language, the savage food, strange clothes, and still stranger ways, with the complete loss of privacy and quiet, and the impossibility of ever relaxing your watchful imitation of the others for months on end, provide such an added stress to the ordinary difficulties of dealing with the Bedu, the climate, and the Turks, that this road should not be chosen without serious thought.

. . . .

The beginning and ending of the secret of handling Arabs is unremitting study of them. Keep always on your guard: never say an inconsidered thing . . . watch yourself and your companions all the time: hear all that passes, search out what is going on beneath the surface, read their characters, discover their tastes and their weaknesses . . . Bury yourself in Arab circles, have no interests and no ideas except the work in hand, so that your brain shall be saturated with one thing only, and you realise your part deeply enough to avoid the little slips that would undo the work of weeks. Your success will be proportioned to the amount of mental effort you devote to it.[6]

By the time Lawrence had worked over his successive manuscripts of the postwar *Seven Pillars* he was able to describe how these theories of his had worked in actual practice. He had followed them himself.

"Since eight copies were required, and the book was very large," T.E. noted, "printing was preferred to typewriting." The Oxford substitute for a typewritten text with carbon copies was the second book he had written with the same title, yet it was only an intermediate stage in a complicated development that would span a decade. Neither it nor the ultimate—and opulent—thirty-guinea Subscription Edition of 1926 was his first published chronicle of the Arab revolt, for as early as the month the war ended—his first weeks back in London—he had drawn on his service notes and his memories for a colorful and often wryly humorous account of the desert campaigns, published anonymously in the *Times* of London in three parts on three days late in November of 1918.[7] He had just given testimony at a meeting of the Eastern Committee of the cabinet and clearly was using the influential *Times* to help mold opinion. The anonymity that was standard *Times* practice was used to advantage by Lawrence, who, still in uniform, was forbidden by army regulations to publish reports concerning his service without authorization. When he published two additional accounts in the *Times* in August, 1920, it was again under the cloak of customary *Times* anonymity.

The trio of 1918 accounts, curiously, flattered the British navy more than Lawrence would in *Seven Pillars*, gave the Turkish regulars more credit for quality than in *Seven Pillars*, praised Feisal for much of the strategy and leadership Lawrence later identified as his own, and announced to London newspaper readers the most "wonderful" of all of Feisal's achievements: "From time immemorial the desert has been a confused and changing mass of blood-feuds and tribal jealousies. To-day there are no blood-feuds among the Arabs from Damascus to Mecca; for the first time in the history of Arabia since the seventh century there is peace along all the pilgrim road." It was a claim for public consumption only, Lawrence knew, for when he had left Damascus only a month earlier, the bitter old tribal jealousies were already creating huge fissures in the veneer of Arab unity which from the start had been a strategic—and artistic—creation of Lawrence's own.

To dramatize the idea of Arab nationhood, Lawrence played down his own role. Telling of an incident which preceded the attack on a Turkish garrison outside Aqaba, he noted that "it was strongly placed. But the Arab leader announced that a sudden darkness at the third night hour would enable it to be rushed without loss—and the moon was good enough to be eclipsed that night. Fortified by such evident proof of ghostly alliance, the Arabs pressed on." In *Seven Pillars* (LIV), T.E. recorded how ibn Jad, the Arab commander assigned to lead the raid, "shrank, made difficulties, pleaded the full moon: but we cut hardly into this excuse, promising that to-night for a while there should be no moon. By my diary there was an eclipse. Duly it came, and the Arabs forced the post without loss, while the superstitious [Turkish] soldiers were firing rifles and clanging copper pots to rescue the threatened satellite."

Similarly, T.E. wrote (anonymously) of the desperate aftermath of the taking of Aqaba:*

> Our position, when we first arrived in Akaba, was miserable. We had no food, and hundreds of prisoners. They ate our riding camels (we killed them two a day), caught fish, and tried to cook the green dates, till the messengers, who had been sent off hastily to Egypt across the Sinai desert, could send help and food by sea. Unfortunately the camels by now had done 1,000 miles in five weeks, and were all jaded, so that it took the men two days to get to Suez, where Admiral Wemyss at once ordered a man-of-war at top speed to Akaba, with all the food that was to be found on the quays. That ship is gratefully remembered in the desert, for it saved 2,000 Arabs and 1,000 Turks from starvation.

In the 1926 *Seven Pillars* (LV), the final stage of the story, it could be told without diplomacy: Time and events had made it unnecessary to conceal the thicket of inefficiency among the sluggish services at Suez, or that the messengers were Lawrence and seven men (who had made the exhausting 150-mile camel march in an extraordinary forty-nine hours), or that it was Admiral Wemyss's subordinate, Burmester, who himself and without consultation ordered the *Dufferin* to load and sail for Aqaba, in order "not to interrupt the Admiral and Allenby."

Other stories, too, were told with deliberate understatement, and each time Lawrence used *we* it was with no indication that the anonymous narrator was anything more than

* Transliteration of place names from the Arabic is inconsistent, even in Lawrence. Except in quotation, current usage is followed (as in Aqaba).

14

an onlooker with mildly lifted eyebrows. On one occasion in the snows of the desert winter, "Sherif Feisal sent out a party of 34 camel riders, to carry money to his brother in Tafileh 80 miles away—and four days afterwards one solitary rider, the only one of the party, struggled in." In *Seven Pillars* (LXXXVIII-LXXXIX) one learns the full drama of the journey ordered not by Feisal but by that solitary survivor—Lawrence. It was all part of a purposeful history.

On July 31, 1919, Lawrence was demobilized as a lieutenant colonel (his war's-end status as a colonel he called "temporary" and "acting") and took advantage of his civilian status to publish his feelings about the peace settlements which seemed likely to be imposed upon the Arabs. But to do so in the *Times* under his own name required his appearance not as an unnamed *Times* reporter but as a letter writer. His letter to the editor, summarizing the controversial wartime documents in which the conflicting promises were made, was written on September 8, 1919. When it was published on September 11, part of the final section about British-Arab agreements had been suppressed by Wickham Steed, the *Times*'s editor. Lawrence had concluded with the afterwards oft-repeated confession that he had been led to believe during the war that his government intended to live up to its (and his) promises to the Arabs; he further admitted that he now regretted what he had said and done because Britain showed no signs of making good on the promises it had authorized him to make when he was seeking Arab support against the Turks.* To further pull the teeth in Lawrence's letter, Wick-

* Yet in *Seven Pillars* Lawrence confessed his disillusionment and dismay in acting in a false role, assuring the Arabs of his government's position while knowing the promises were hollow. He had deliberately treated General Barrow, who reached Deraa after the Arabs, as their "guest," and he stalled General Chauvel so that the Arabs might enter Damascus first in the hope of assuring their claim to some part of Arabia.

ham Steed accompanied it by a *Times* editorial which blandly supported the government's position. Still it is easy to understand why Lawrence would have contributed again anonymously to the *Times* the next year, for he must have valued covert and subtle propagandizing as opposed to overt, signed letters which were susceptible to censorship. The *Times* was the most influential shopwindow in England for his cause.

The next year, when events were going badly for Feisal and for both the British and the Arabs in Mesopotamia (Iraq), Lawrence again wanted declarations published prominently under his own name. This time he used the pages of the *Daily Express* (May 28 and 29, 1920), the *Sunday Times* (May 30, 1920), and the *Observer* (August 8, 1920), as well as the *Times*.* (For the *Express* pieces Lawrence would take no payment, and the editor sent him—after some search—a gift copy of a rare edition of *The Arabian Nights*.) From Baghdad, the Arabophile English traveler and civil servant Gertrude Bell, a longtime friend of Lawrence, wrote (addressing him as "Beloved boy"), "I've been reading with amusement your articles in the papers; what curious organs you choose for self expression! However whatever the organs I'm largely in agreement with what you say."

In his ringing public letters it was not a different Lawrence but a different writer who appeared under his signature, for his polemic prose was simple, forceful, and direct, unlike the circumlocutions of his introspective writings. Yet he must have realized as early as his appearances at Versailles in 1919

---

* There was even a newspaper piece published under Lawrence's name by mistake. He had offered to try to place an article by his old friend S. F. Newcombe in a London daily and used his influence successfully. The reason soon became obvious: when the article appeared in October, 1920, in the *Daily Telegraph* it was erroneously printed under Lawrence's signature.

that for all his personal fame and argumentative talents, his war of words on behalf of the Arabs he once briefly thought he had freed was doomed to be lost. Britain would not endanger her relationship with France over the issue of independence for the peoples of the former Ottoman Empire.

In December, 1919, the first of his signed memoir-pieces appeared but went almost entirely unnoticed, for it had been published in the *Royal Engineer's Journal*, hardly a mass-circulation London newspaper. Although it contained material Lawrence was later to use in the final version of *Seven Pillars*, "Demolitions Under Fire" was for the most part an admirable technical article in lucid, precise prose suitable for the medium. Only rarely did the author betray his literary pretensions. It must have struck the ordnance and engineer officers who read the article as strange to discover such a comment about one particularly effective system of track demolition as "The appearance of a piece of rail treated by this method is most beautiful, for the sleepers rise up in all manner of varied forms, like the early buds of tulips."

For raw material Lawrence had apparently gone back to the last and longest of his *Arab Bulletin* reports, published in Cairo as Bulletin No. 106 and concluding with the entry into Damascus. In a footnote he had explained his "tulip system" of laying demolition charges much as one would plant bulbs. "The effect of a long stretch of line planted with these 'tulips' is most beautiful," he had written, "since no two look just alike." He had preserved his metaphor and afterwards provided a more literary treatment for it.

To recover copies of the *Arab Bulletin*[8] and handwritten notes and reports he had left behind, which he now needed for his book, he had followed his futile efforts in Paris with the disastrous flight to Cairo which almost cost him his life. He understood the potential of air travel as well as air warfare, but the flight (one of many which crashed), rather than saving him weeks, cost him months of hospitalization and recuperation. Of the fifty-one twin-engined bombers which had left Lille in April, 1919, only twenty-six had made it to Egypt by October. Within forty-eight hours of his arrival in Cairo he was on his way back—again by air. It was not all wasted time: he was more convinced than ever that he wanted to have a role in the air force's future, and he returned with both the material he needed to expand his ideas into a book on the Arab revolt and an introduction to it already written.

By the time Lawrence's 1920 *Times* articles building up Feisal appeared, he had not only completed a manuscript version of *Seven Pillars* but had apparently written most of it twice. In a postscript to a letter to Charles Doughty written November 25, 1919, he confided, "I lost the MS. of my own adventure in Arabia: it was stolen from me in the train." The manuscript had been carried in a bag similar to those used by bank messengers and must have caused great disappointment to the purloiner when he opened it. In any event, the nearly completed draft was never recovered, and Lawrence applied his already legendary energy and self-discipline to reconstruct from his reports, notes, previously published articles— and memory—a new first draft, usually referred to as a second version.*

---

* "I wrote Books 2, 3, 4, 5, 6, 7 and 10 in Paris between February and June of 1919. The introduction was written between Paris and Egypt on my way out to Cairo by Handley-Page [bomber] in July and August 1919. Afterwards in England I wrote Book 1: and then lost all but the Introduction and drafts of Books 9 and 10 at Reading Station, while changing trains. This was about

There was no shortage of available personal documentary material. He had the two wartime diaries he had kept, although, as in most other modern conflicts before and since, there were futile service prohibitions against keeping a diary. From laconic entries he would later not only reconstruct the chronology of his movements but extrapolate vivid scenes. One such notation—"camel dead calf, suffering over skin"— referred to the death of the foal of Lawrence's Ghazala ("the old grandmother camel, now magnificently fit"). Frugally, his personal attendant Abdullah, had skinned the carcass and carried the dry pelt behind his saddle, "like a crupper piece," until:

After an hour Ghazala lifted her head high, and began to pace uneasily, picking up her feet like a sword-dancer. I tried to urge her: but Abdulla dashed alongside me, swept his cloak about him, and sprung from his saddle, calf's skin in hand. He lighted with a splash of gravel in front of Ghazala, who had come to a standstill, gently moaning. On the ground before her he spread the little hide, and drew her head down to it. She stopped crying, shuffled its dryness thrice with her lips; then again lifted her head and, with a whimper, strode forward. Several times in the day this happened; but afterwards she seemed to forget. (XCIX)

There were also, T.E. told Robert Graves, "some other route-sheets, with descriptive notes of what happened on the march, daily, and rough compass-bearings and march-hours. The Wejh-Aqaba notes are amongst them, and Wejh-Wadi Ais-Aba el Naam and back. These are detailed. They contain e.g., the full text of the tribal feast chapter [XLVI in the Subscription Edition] almost verbatim. It was with them, and

Christmas, 1919." (Lawrence, in the four-page leaflet, *Some Notes on the Writing of The Seven Pillars of Wisdom* by T. E. Shaw, presented to those who received the 1926 edition.)

with the reports in the *Arab Bulletin*, that I reinforced and pegged down my memory."*

Much of the new manuscript was written during weeks spent in an attic hermitage in Barton Street, Westminster, in space borrowed from his architect-friend Sir Herbert Baker. Alone—and deliberately so—Lawrence forced himself into what might now be called a "mind-expanding" state, exciting his imagination "with hunger and cold and sleeplessness," he thought, "more than de Quincey with his opium." Explaining his method (but ignoring the considerable mass of preliminary material he had as foundation) he wrote, "I tie myself into knots trying to reenact everything, as I write it out. It's like writing in front of a looking-glass, and never looking at the paper, but always at the imaginary scene."

Cultivating the writer-in-the-garret image, T.E. afterwards included in his itinerary for Robert Graves's book about him the statement "London all 1920." Yet his July, 1920, letter to the *Times* was dated from All Souls, as were private letters he sent from January through November; and Graves, the anonymous author[9] of the "Isis Idol" feature in the Oxonian *Isis*, reported in a 1920 column about Lawrence ("Of Arabia and All Souls"):

When I arrived I found my Idol sound asleep in bed, at eleven-thirty in the morning. A college scout informed me that this is no sign of sloth; our Idol is not one of the race of men celebrated in the psalm; he does not rise at dawn and go about his long labour until the evening; he is, on the contrary, one with the lions roaring in the night season. He has discarded Eastern dress and often wears trousers, he writes chatty letters to *The Times* with

* Some of the terse diary entries correspond closely to portions of *Seven Pillars*, notably in Chapters x, xviii–xix, xxiii, xxxviii, and lix. In rare cases the tone is different, perhaps as a result of the impact of time and distance. Extracts from the diaries were published by A. W. Lawrence in *Secret Despatches from Arabia* (London, 1939).

the regularity of an old clubman, and has even been known to dine in college.

Graves had first met Lawrence in Oxford in those years, when the poet was an out-of-place war-veteran student. It was late in the winter of 1920, Graves recalled in *Good-Bye to All That*, and T.E.—resplendent in full evening dress—was chatting with visitors at an All Souls "guest-night," including the Regius Professor of Divinity, to whom T.E. spoke of the influence of the Syrian-Greek philosophers on early Christianity. Graves became a regular morning visitor to Lawrence's memorabilia-cluttered rooms—"but not before eleven o'clock or half-past, because he worked at night, going to bed at dawn." They avoided talk of the war and, "though the long, closely-written foolscap sheets of *The Seven Pillars* were always stacked in a neat pile on his living room table," Graves restrained his curiosity. Instead they talked of poets and prose writers they admired, including Hardy and Doughty. "When I asked Doughty," T.E. told Graves, "why he had made that Arabian journey his answer was that he had gone there 'to redeem the English language from the slough into which it has fallen since the time of Spenser.'" The words, Graves thought, had a profound impact upon Lawrence and accounted, largely, "for his furious keying-up of style in *The Seven Pillars*."

The "keying-up of style" seemed to be cumulative, increasing with the intensity of Lawrence's preoccupation with successive stages of the manuscript, and with the distance in time from the events it described. Some of the evidence for this metamorphosis in manner appeared in print as, from time to time, he drew material from a current draft for an immediate use. One opportunity had come when Guy Dawnay, a

21

colonel when Lawrence had served with him in the Middle East, asked T.E. for a piece for the inaugural (October, 1920) issue of the *Army Quarterly*. "I had my account of the Arab Revolt by me," he recalled later to military affairs writer Liddell Hart, "and boiled down two chapters of it (excising some sections, I fancy) into a review article. I can't remember whether I recast any part of it. Possible." He had no copy of the final (subscription) *Seven Pillars* by him, but guessed that material in the *Quarterly* article did later turn up in that version: "I think that a puzzlement about the general principles of war came about page 100, when I was ill in Abdullah's camp: and that some notes on tactics came later, about page 350, after Akaba had been captured." The guess to Liddell Hart was accurate. Material he had utilized from the developing new draft to construct "The Evolution of a Revolt" appeared in its final state in Chapters XXXIII, XXXVIII, and LIX of *Seven Pillars*.

Liddell Hart had written in his capacity as military editor of the fourteenth edition of the *Encyclopaedia Britannica*, (1929) asking T.E. to do an article on guerrilla warfare but suggesting that if Lawrence (then, in 1927, Aircraftman Shaw, at a base in India) could not manage a fresh article, the 1920 "Evolution of a Revolt" might serve. T.E., not interested in preparing a new piece, agreed that the *Britannica* could have the *Army Quarterly* article, but suggested a sounder alternative—that Liddell Hart boil the article down to its essentials, and fill it out with pertinent reflections from other places in the final text: "You are at liberty to quote from the *Seven Pillars* any paragraphs dealing with general theories of war, or application of these theories, or any tactical disquisitions." As a result the *Britannica*'s section on "Guerrilla

Warfare"—in which Lawrence had no more hand than that—
appeared above the initials T.E.L.*

Lawrence's analysis of "irregular war"—and his easy, yet
scholarly, references to both classic and modern theoreticians
of tactics—had appealed to Liddell Hart, although there may
have also been in the back of his mind the sense of *coup* to be
achieved in eliciting a contribution over T.E.'s initials. Retro-
spectively, the piece has additional interest, for although it
was written before Lawrence's enlistment as a private, it
contains not only a donnish survey of guerrilla strategy but a
probing into the psychology of the ranks:

We had no discipline, in the sense in which it is restrictive, submergent
of individuality, the lowest common denominator of men. In regular armies
in peace it means the limit of energy attainable by everybody present: it is
the hunt not of an average, but of an absolute, a 100-per-cent standard, in
which the ninety-nine stronger men are played down to the level of the
worst. The aim is to render the unit a unit, and the man a type, in order that
their effort shall be calculable, their collective output even in grain and in
bulk. The deeper the discipline, the lower the individual efficiency, and the
more sure the performance. It is a deliberate sacrifice of capacity in order to
reduce the uncertain element, the bionomic factor, in enlisted humanity,
and its accompaniment is *compound* or social war, that form in which the
man in the fighting line has to be the product of the multipled exertions of
the long hierarchy, from workshop to supply unit, which maintains him in
the field.

The subject was one Lawrence would weave with fascinated

* "Evolution of a Revolt" had some additional influence outside T.E.'s own
writings. In John Buchan's novel *Courts of the Morning* (1929)—first titled in
manuscript "Far Arabia"—Sandy Arbuthnot, a master of disguises and derring-
do, leads a guerrilla-style "South American" insurrection, cutting railways,
staging hit-and-run raids, and living off the land. Arbuthnot describes his tactics
and strategy in terms strikingly like "Evolution of a Revolt," which Buchan had
read in 1927 while working on his novel. ("I should greatly like to see Lawrence's article on Guerrilla Warfare reprinted," Buchan had written to Liddell
Hart on October 1, 1927.) [Janet Adam Smith, *John Buchan* (Boston, 1965),
262]

interest into his posthumously published service chronicle, *The Mint*.

The manuscript from which "Evolution of a Revolt" evolved did not satisfy Lawrence; but before he abandoned it, early in 1921, he developed from it an eight-chapter abridgment. From July through October, 1921, four of the parts (II, III, IV, and VIII) were published in the New York–based current affairs magazine *The World's Work*,* while Lawrence was back in the Middle East intermittently on Colonial Office business. Chapter II, in the manuscript entitled "A Set-Back, December, 1916," became "With Feisal at Court and Afield. I. Adventures in Arabia with the Prince of the Hedjaz and the Desert Tribes." Chapter III, "Experiments, March 1917," became "Arabian Nights and Days: A Second Chapter from a Hitherto Unpublished Personal Record of the Arab Revolt and Conflicts with the Turks." "A Camel Charge, July 1917," received the expanded title of "Arabian Nights and Days. III. A Camel Charge, and Other Adventures in the Desert." The eighth chapter of the manuscript, "The Turkish Army Passes, September 1918," became the fourth and final part of *The World's Work* series as "Adventures in Arabia's Deliverance: The Turkish Army Passes." They were, T.E. wrote Robert Graves, "literal extracts from a book I wrote: but all the personal (subjective) part is left out for

---

* Frank Nelson Doubleday, whose firm owned *The World's Work*, had met Lawrence early in 1919 at the Paris Peace Conference, introduced by Rudyard Kipling. Eager to get a Lawrence of Arabia piece for his magazine, Doubleday suggested that T.E. write something, "which he did, and handed it to me. I told him that it was very good, but suggested that he should add to it and make it a little longer. He said that he would do this and took it away with him. When next I saw him he told me that he thought it was no good and he had destroyed it." F. N. Doubleday, *The Memoirs of a Publisher* (New York, 1972), was written in 1926 (see pp. 255–56). What *The World's Work* published nearly three years later was obviously something else.

dignity's sake." Although a thousand pounds had once been offered for the publication rights, the proceeds amounted to only two hundred pounds, for Lawrence had Graves make the sale and pocket the proceeds. The young poet was in desperate financial difficulties, and T.E. wanted no personal gain from a work he still considered unpresentable and unpublishable. Profitless and flamboyantly advertised publication across the Atlantic in New York apparently did not count: for Lawrence the publishing world was London.

Again, the text is useful in assessing the trend toward heightened "literary" and dramatic effects, some apparently products of a creative imagination rather than corrections in a chronicle. Paragraphs in parallel evidence the transition. The paragraph on the left is taken from the second part of *The World's Work* series (based on the second text); that on the right is from Chapter xxxiv of the 1926 text.

The shepherd lad kept on steadily and drove his goats with shrill cries up our hill. The best pasture was on the top and down the western side. Hussein, one of our men, moved behind the ridge along which the boy must come, and as soon as he was safe from observation from the station, jumped out and caught him. The lad was a Heteimi, one of those outcasts of the desert, members of no recognized Arab stock, whose children commonly

The shepherd lad held on steadily, driving his goats with shrill cries up our hill for the better pasture on the western side. We sent two Juheina down behind a ridge beyond sight of the enemy, and they ran from each side and caught him. The lad was of the outcast Heteym, pariahs of the desert, whose poor children were commonly sent on hire as shepherds to the tribes about them. This one cried continually, and made efforts to escape hire themselves out as herds to the tribes about them. He cried continually, and made efforts to escape from us whenever he saw one of his flock straying uncared for about the hill, so that in the end the men lost patience and tied him up tightly. Fauzan tried to talk to him, but all his anxiety was for his goats, and he could tell us nothing about his Turkish masters.

as often as he saw his goats straying uncared-for about the hill. In the end the men lost patience and tied him up roughly, when he screamed for terror that they would kill him. Fauzan had great ado to make him quiet, and then questioned him about his Turkish masters. But all his thoughts were for the flock: his eyes followed them miserably while the tears made edged and crooked tracks down his dirty face.

Some of the later changes would attempt to elevate the language, often at the price of saltiness, wryness, or directness. Some would strive for a Doughty-like archaism of language. "The tracks of the others were easy to follow," he wrote in the same section of the 1921 text, later "improving" it to "A band of trodden untidiness in a sweep of gleaming water-rounded sand showed us the way." In some cases concision in the narrative was the inevitable result, for later versions, even where more verbiage was used to say something, were thousands of words shorter in total length. As a result the early texts often have the added value of having retained narrative elements later abandoned. One learns, for example, what eventually happened to the little Heteimi shepherd boy who, in the interest of narrative pace, disappears more quickly from the Subscription Edition than from the earlier text:

We rode straight back to Abdulla's camp which we reached on April the first. Shakir, who is splendid in habit, held a grand parade, and thousands of joy-shots were fired in honor of his victory. I found the little Heteimi lad a billet as shepherd to Dakhil Allah, Mohammed's father. This consoled him for losing his former place without a reference, and his consolation was turned into active joy when we gave him a new shirt and a colored head cloth. He asked for the kindness of a rifle thrown in!

In some cases, although the narrative remained essentially unchanged, the transitions in word-choice altered the sense of drama in, or the tone of, an incident. Earlier, one of the Ageyli is pulled out of a well "very wet and frightened." Later he is "very wet and angry." When Lawrence, amid a mob of well-meaning tribesmen, searches in the darkness for the hair-trigger to two mines "so powerful that they would have rooted up fifty yards of the bank," he is "glad I was insured." Later the charges are estimated to be "so powerful that they would have rooted out seventy yards of track," and the task "seemed, at the time, an almost uninsurable occupation." If the charges had gone off then and wiped out the entire force of irregulars swarming about the trackage within sight of the puzzled enemy, Lawrence concluded cleanly and wryly, "To be sure that would have completed the Turks' bewilderment." For the final version Lawrence succumbed to the temptation of artifice. "To be sure," he rewrote the line, "such a feat would have properly completed the bewilderment of the Turks!"

More curious even than the changes in word-choice is the additional narrative material published at the close of the incident in which Lawrence (in the third of *The World's Work* parts and Chapter LIV of the Subscription Edition) goes down at night into the valley to view the enemy dead:

27

The dead lay naked under
the moon. Turks are much
whiter-skinned than the
Arabs among whom I had
been living, and these
were mere boys. Close
around them lapped the
dark wormwood, now heavy
with dew and sparkling
like sea spray. Wearied
in mind and body, I felt
that I would rather be
of this quiet company
than with the shouting
restless mob farther
up the valley, boasting
of their speed and
strength, and
quarrelling over the
plunder. For, however
this campaign might go
with its unforeseen
toils and pains, death
must be the last
chapter in the history
of every man of us.

The dead men looked
wonderfully beautiful.
The night was shining
gently down, softening
them into new ivory.
Turks were white-skinned
on their clothed parts,
much whiter than the Arabs;
and these soldiers had
been very young. Close
round them lapped the dark
wormwood, now heavy with
dew, in which the ends of
the moonbeams sparkled
like seaspray. The corpses
seemed flung so pitifully
on the ground, huddled
anyhow in low heaps.
Surely if straightened
they would be comfortable
at last. So I put them all
in order, one by one, very
wearied myself, and longing
to be of these quiet ones,
not of the restless, noisy,
aching mob up the valley,
quarrelling over the
plunder, boasting of their
speed and strength to
endure God knew how many
toils and pains of this
sort; with death, whether
we won or lost, waiting
to end the history.

The remainder of the 40,000-word abridgment ("10% of
the whole," T.E. called it) was never published but did survive, although Lawrence used a blowtorch to destroy the

manuscript from which it was drawn.[10] By then it had been superseded by yet another version, based on earlier writings but even more self-consciously "literary." Confessing as much, he wrote:

Probably something should be said of the peculiarities of this draft. For the style of telling is owed a special apology. As a great reader of books, my own language has been made up of choosing from the black heap of words those which much-loved men have stooped to, and charged with rich meaning, and made our living possession. Everywhere there are such borrowed phrases and ideas, not picked out by footnotes and untidy quotation marks, since great lords of thought must be happy to see us tradesmen setting up our booths under their castle-walls and dealing in their struck coinage.*

The 330,000 words—crowded into an accountant's ledger from Herbert Baker's office—were written during Lawrence's service with the Colonial Office in London and in the Middle East. The manuscript was begun (T.E. noted in the ledger) on September 1, 1920, and completed on May 9, 1922. It was this rhetorically inflated text—slightly revised as it was set—which he had printed at the Oxford *Times* printing plant, beginning on January 20, 1922, even before he had completed the writing. On June 24 the last pages of his eight-copy edition came off the press. Three of them were afterwards destroyed in the process of creating his final text.

The complex creative history of *Seven Pillars* was far from over when Lawrence lent his first copy to Rudyard Kipling and then to Bernard Shaw, for it was this Oxford version that Shaw and Lawrence pruned (about 13 percent of the text) and revised into the famous 127-copy† Subscription Edition of

* These lines were cut from the 1926 text and from the posthumous 1936 trade edition.

† In addition Lawrence gave away to friends at least sixty-two additional copies, some of which he considered incomplete.

1926, and from which the 130,000-word abridgment *Revolt in the Desert* (1927) was taken. Lawrence's major claim to literary significance, his attempt at a modern epic, has had many incarnations.

CHAPTER II

Seven Pillars of Wisdom
and Revolt in the Desert

GREAT writers, from Cervantes to Lawrence of Arabia, Hugh Walpole has written, "have been amateur writers, and the literature of the world would be poorer without them. . . . One unique book is enough for an author's survival . . . because there will never be again in the history of man any rival to them . . . but especially because they reveal so clearly the unique personality of their writers, men all of a certain sturdiness and independence. They are also men who have written because they must, who have learned in no schools and been afraid of no criticism."[1] Men of deeds seldom need to search for the substitute of words and, when impelled or inspired to write, often remain the author of that single book. Should that book spawn successors, they are often only the same book under a variety of guises and titles. Their unique limitations arise, Denis de Rougemont suggests, because such authors are seldom "born writers" who possess not only talent but ease and dexterity. Rather:

They have formed themselves in a world where error involves immediate sanctions, where exactitude is vital, whether in drafting an order or commanding a technical operation. These scruples over subduing the precise meaning to rhythm or the play of syllables can spoil the movement of a text: They do not care. The best of them compensate on a profounder level of linguistic effectiveness: Certain formulas to manipulate minds, and especially to impose a determined angle of vision upon them—which is the whole secret of command—are either known to them or instinctive. It is not only to their reputations as adventurers, revolutionaries, or aviators that the particular prestige of their writings is due but as much to the effectiveness of a syntax which knows how to "take hold."[2]

Lawrence may have been that kind of writer. Unquestionably he loved lingering over the discriminating choice of an adjective and found joy in stylistic changes which would have tortured the patience of practiced writers.

The changes in which Lawrence found no pleasure were those predicated upon political or legal considerations. To effect the excision or modification of passages in *Seven Pillars* which were, warned Bernard Shaw, possibly libelous and certainly politically questionable, G.B.S. had to recommend such changes on purely literary grounds. As a result, late in the summer of 1924, after Lawrence's printer Manning Pike had delivered the first page-proofs of the revised subscription text, G.B.S. blue-penciled the entire first chapter, rationalizing that the second chapter made a better beginning than the first. Shaw grounded his decision on the comparative effectiveness of the "furious rush of words" opening the second chapter, compared with the personal and political introspection of the first. This becomes clear in the notes G.B.S. added years later to the flyleaf of Charlotte's subscription copy. The opening chapter "was a record of the stirring of his [Lawrence's] very sickly conscience (Ibsen's phrase) instead of establishing, as in a play, the who and when and where and how and what which readers must know if they are to understand what they are reading. He accepted this."[3] The first seven chapters were immediately renumbered to reflect the excision, which, despite Shaw's regular denials, seems to have had a political as well as a literary basis. Shaw apparently felt that it was neither tasteful nor politic for Lawrence to open his epic with a declaration of his disillusionment with British and French Machiavellian diplomacy, especially since it seemed prudent to be on good terms with a government which T.E. then hoped would restore him to the R.A.F.

Pointing to the contradictory nature of statements in the introductory chapter in which Lawrence insisted upon the subjective nature of his history, Jean Beraud Villars, writing from the perspective of a Frenchman who felt that France was unduly abused, suggested that Shaw recognized that "these preliminary statements would remove all credence from the work." Villars deplored the chapter's posthumous publication.* To him it was a naïve gesture and was "to the great concern of future historians."

Work on the revision continued through 1924 and 1925, with Lawrence insisting all the while on the importance of the appearance of the printed page. Like G.B.S. he disapproved of too much white space, particularly "rivers" in the type, like broad cracks running down the page. Both men gave way to William Morris–inspired enthusiasm for the book beautiful, but Lawrence went even further than G.B.S., choosing to alter what he had to say, if necessary, to achieve the appearance he insisted the page have. His specifications included

---

* The suppressed chapter, bitter and sad, was first published in a posthumous miscellany of Lawrence's writings, *Oriental Assembly* (1939), and appears in editions of *Seven Pillars* now in print.

a page of a uniform thirty-seven lines, each page beginning with a new paragraph. Most pages had to begin with an ornamental capital so that when the book lay open its two pages would balance in appearance. The last line of each page had to be solid, with the last lines of other paragraphs running beyond the middle of the line, again to avoid blocks of white space. Words were not to be split at the ends of lines, and every chapter had to end at the bottom right-hand corner. "Incredible meticulousness," Vyvyan Richards later wrote, "—reducing all writing to an absurdity—it really seems. But there is almost no trace of these Procrustean games in the actual text—he had an amazing command of word and phrase. The most careful reader of the later popular edition, where, of course, all this typographical precision is dropped, would never suspect that the text had been so forced." Each alteration meant more rearrangement by Lawrence to satisfy his aesthetic principles, but the slow pace of service life gave him plenty of time.

Another critical crotchet asserted itself when the book reached galley-proof stage, and T.E. began to prepare what was proving to be an endless index to the volume. Giving up the drudgery, he provided instead a twelve-page, book-by-book and chapter-by-chapter synopsis, as well as a rationalization both for what he had prepared and for what he had not.

Half-way through the labour of an index to this book, I recalled the practice of my ten years' study of history; and realized I had never used the index of a book fit to read. Who would insult his *Decline and Fall*, by consulting it just upon a specific point? I am aware that my achievement as a writer falls short of every conception of the readable; but surely not so far as to make it my duty ... to save readers the pain of an unnecessary page. The contents seem to me adequately finger-posted by this synopsis.

The argument could hold no water with serious students of history, in Lawrence's time as well as before and since. But *Seven Pillars* had to wait for posthumous editions to acquire an index.

As the summer of 1924 drifted on, T.E.—now a private in the tank corps—found his storeman-clerk's job ideal for reading proof, while Pike, with an assistant, worked in a reconverted shop near Paddington Station, setting type by machine and adjusting and readjusting each page. September was the month for Pike's vacation in Cornwall, and when pages of proof stopped coming in to Lawrence, T.E. forwarded all he had on hand (forty pages) to the Shaws, with the injection to "Please alter, mark, erase, add, abuse anything which hits you: either technical, or literary, or moral, or intellectual." The extent of the changes was beyond his expectations, and when the proof was returned to him he admitted to being staggered with more than gratitude. In the middle of October he confessed to Sydney Cockerell that G.B.S. had read the proof and "left not a paragraph without improvement . . . but some nearly died in the operation. Not a trace of anaesthetic! Bracing of him to treat me by his standard."[4]

A sample (in parallel) of both texts, where the alterations were modest, demonstrates the predominantly stylistic nature of the revisions:

[Oxford text]	[Subscription Edition]
The Muadhins began to send their call through the warm moist night over the feasting and illuminations of the	Later I was sitting alone in my room, working and thinking out as firm a way as the turbulent memories of the day allowed, when the

city. From a little mosque quite near there was one who cried into my open window, a man with a ringing voice of special sweetness, and I found myself involuntarily distinguishing his words: "God alone is great. I testify that there is no god but God, and Mohammed the Prophet of God. Come to prayer. Come to security. God alone is great. There is no god but God."

At the close he dropped his voice two tones, almost to speaking level, and very softly added, "And he is very good to us this day, O people of Damascus." The clamour beneath him hushed suddenly, as everyone seemed to obey the call to prayer for the first night in their lives of perfect freedom; while my fancy showed me in the overwhelming pause my loneliness and lack of reason in their movement, since only for me of the tens of thousands in the city was that phrase meaningless.

Muedhdhins began to send their call of last prayer through the moist night over the illuminations of the feasting city. One, with a ringing voice of special sweetness, cried into my window from a near mosque. I found myself involuntarily distinguishing his words: "God alone is great: I testify there are no gods, but God: and Mohammed his Prophet. Come to prayer: come to security. God alone is great: there is no god—but God."

At the close he dropped his voice two tones, almost to speaking level, and softly added: "And He is very good to us this day, O people of Damascus." The clamour hushed, as everyone seemed to obey the call to prayer on this their first night of perfect freedom. While my fancy, in the overwhelming pause, showed me my loneliness and lack of reason in their movement: since only for me, of all the hearers, was the event sorrowful and the phrase meaningless.

Revisions were made in all four categories Lawrence had enumerated, as well as in that delicate fifth—political. Linguistic excesses were tempered; attacks upon British duplicity in the Middle East were softened or cut (chief reason for removal of the first chapter); and overexplicit and—sympathetic—analyses of rampant Arab homosexuality were toned down or excised (chief reason for removal of a later chapter) in hopes of forestalling any misconstruing of Lawrence's own essentially asexual nature.

Asexual by no means meant *inexperienced*, for sexual experience came to Lawrence—if not sooner—violently and perversely in the notorious episode he recounted dramatically but discreetly in Chapter LXXX of the Subscription Edition. Captured while on a spying mission near Deraa, he was homosexually abused and beaten by Hajim, the Bey of Deraa. Apparently unrecognized, he was then thrown into the street and painfully made his way back to friendly lines; but "the passing days confirmed . . . how in Deraa that night the citadel of my integrity had been irrevocably lost." The motives for his reaction to the humiliation and defilement—self-deprivation of glory and self-punishment thereafter—would have been more clear to the few privileged readers of the Oxford narrative than to the still-few readers of the 1926 edition, for Lawrence dropped the most introspective passage about his own sexuality—the original last passage of the chapter, in which he had crept out of Deraa, "as though some part of me had gone dead that night . . . leaving me maimed, imperfect, only half myself. It could not have been the defilement, for no one ever held the body in less honour than I did myself. Probably it had been the breaking of the spirit by that frenzied, nerve-shattering pain which had degraded me to the beast level when it made me grovel to it, and which had journeyed with me since, a fascination and terror and morbid desire, lascivious and vicious perhaps, but like the striving of a moth toward its flame."*

Carnality of any kind was repellent to Lawrence and had been so apparently since he had discovered that he had been conceived in illegality and sin; after Deraa he could be sympathetic to the weakness in men that required some form of coupling, but he realized that such sympathies could be misplaced and misunderstood in public print. In his *Some Notes on the Writing of The Seven Pillars of Wisdom*, T.E. referred to the homosexual encounter excised from Chapter LXXXIV as that "unpleasantly unnecessary incident." It concerned an Arab and an Englishman among the troops discovered in sodomy. The Arab was summarily sentenced by his tribal leaders to one hundred lashes—the punishment recommended by the Prophet—but Lawrence managed to secure a reduction to fifty strokes with the cane. The British soldier, although placed under arrest for later court-martial, was snatched from custody by his comrades and given fifty strokes plus ten, after which the punishment was reported to Lawrence, who

---

* Much has been written about Lawrence as a possible homosexual, and particularly as a masochist, the self-punishing aspects of *Seven Pillars* and *The Mint* being undoubtedly a reflection of his pathology. The most convincing statement in print is that of David Garnett, editor of Lawrence's letters, in a note to author T. H. White, who was a homosexual. "T. E. Lawrence wasn't a homosexual. I know that for a fact as I have read a correspondence which I could not publish between him and a friend who was a homosexual. Lawrence may even have wished he were one. He was a masochist, in the strict sense of the word." [David Garnett (ed.), *The White-Garnett Letters* (New York, 1968), 308.] Lawrence's postwar masochism, which involved hiring a Scots youth named John Bruce early in 1922 to inflict ritual floggings, has been established by Philip Knightley and Colin Simpson in *The Secret Lives of Lawrence of Arabia* (1970); however the aberration has no traceable literary impact.

meditates in the chapter about the emotional pressures under which men without women lived. He hushed up the incident. It was not possible to tolerate among Englishmen what isolation and desert heat made endemic among Arabs who, despite Mohammed's injunction, won Lawrence's sympathy by a "spiritual union" that was more than "the attraction of flesh to flesh." In a letter from his barracks to Lionel Curtis on May 27, 1923, he explained that "surely the world would be more clean" if procreation were unnecessary, yet "You wouldn't exist, I wouldn't exist, without this carnality. . . . Isn't it true that the fault of birth rests somewhat on the child? I believe it's we who led our parents on to bear us, and it's our unborn children who made our flesh itch. A filthy business all of it." The heterosexual itch that brought T.E. into sinful and illegitimate being and a world of pain revolted him more than the homosexual couplings he had described tolerantly in the earlier versions of *Seven Pillars*. But he understood the climate in which his book would be published. Sexual reticence was even more crucial than political reticence.

Although politics dictated the dropping of his opening chapter, T.E. mourned its utter loss, especially since the second page contained his Homeric catalogue of names—those figuring in the event to whom he wished to pay homage. Rather than protest the excision, he decided to include the names elsewhere. Eventually they, too, found their way into the brief preface. There were also modifications in his criticism of a number of English military leaders mentioned under their own names—the result of concern about libel or the lessening of his emotional involvement. And there was a large cut—"an abortive reconnaissance." But the book was much too long and had to be kept to reasonable size. Pages had to be measured in pounds rather than shillings.

Not only the words had to be paid for; the illustrations would cost more than the text. Even at thirty guineas a copy, the project would not pay for itself, and Lawrence began reconsidering the commercial version he had once scorned. A popular edition of an abridged text would meet the rising expenses. An agreement for "War in the Desert" ("War" became "Revolt" later) was drawn up, calling for delivery of a 120,000-word manuscript by March 31, 1926, and an advance of three thousand pounds. The book turned out to be slightly larger, although Lawrence said half-seriously that he made the abridgment by cutting out every other paragraph. An earlier abridgment made by Edward Garnett he ignored completely. Using a set of Subscription Edition sheets, a brush, india ink, and a wastebasket, he began by throwing away the first seven chapters. Other cuts involved removing consecutive pages, and whole chapters, elsewhere. It was a crude piece of work, made to keep the necessary readjustments to a minimum and to reduce the need for writing new material to those places where it was otherwise impossible to see the shortened version's "real shape across the gaps."

Beginning with his arrival in Arabia (Chapter VIII in the original), Lawrence concentrated on action rather than introspection—action, at that, of a variety likely to be approved by middle-class morality. Thus the dedicatory poem disappears, and the introductory and magisterial passages on the origins of the Arab revolt are eliminated, as are the chapters on nationalism (XIV), on Lawrence's excruciating execution of the Arab (XXXI), on his illness and his developing a theory of

guerrilla warfare (XXXII–XXXIII), on the arranging of the
dead (LII), on the origins of Christianity (LXIII), on Lawrence's capture and torture at Deraa (LXXX), on sex and discipline (XCII), on his guilt feelings about deception of the
Arabs (C and CIII), and on the graphic horror of the Turkish
hospital in Damascus (CXXI). The symbolic concluding chapter (CXXII) was also cut. Inevitably it was an inferior work,
although it captured much of the excitement of the original.
In the process of cutting, the personal and subjective—the
heart of the book—disappeared, replaced, as Lawrence wrote
Forster, by "unity and speed and compactness."

Where pace was impeded by color, the color was eliminated also. From the 652 pages of the original printed text,
211 were eliminated altogether; and in the end several new
paragraphs were needed to provide continuity where the ex-
cisions were wholesale, a task made more difficult toward the
end when, in March, 1926, Lawrence broke his wrist and had
to pencil in his linkages left-handed. For the most part Lawrence's method is illustrated by a sample page from the Subscription Edition (Chapter VIII), the lines through the words
indicating his own instructions, boldly slashed across the
sheets in india ink:

Just north of Jidda was a second group of black-white buildings, moving
up and down like pistons in the mirage, as the ship rolled at anchor and the
intermittent wind shifted the heat waves in the air. ~~It looked and felt horrible. We began to regret that the inaccessibility which made the Hejaz
militarily a safe theatre of revolt involved bad climate and un wholesome-
ness.~~

~~However,~~ Colonel Wilson, British representative with the new Arab
state, had sent his launch to meet us; and we had to go ashore to learn the
reality of the men levitating in that mirage. ~~Half an hour later Ruhi, Con-
sular Oriental assistant, was grinning a delighted welcome to his old patron
Storrs, (Ruhi, the ingenious, more like a mandrake than a man), while the~~

~~newly appointed Syrian police and harbour officers, with a scratch guard of honour, lined the Customs Wharf in salutation of Aziz el Masri. Sherif Abdulla, the second son of the old man of Mecca, was reported just arriving in the town. He it was we had to meet; so our coming was auspiciously timed.~~

We walked past the white masonry of the still-building water gate, and through the oppressive alley of the food market on our way to the Consulate. In the air, from the men to the dates and back to the meat, squadrons of flies like particles of dust danced up and down the sunshafts which stabbed into the darkest corners of the booths through torn places in the wood and sackcloth awnings overhead. The atmosphere was like a bath. ~~The scarlet leathers of the armchair on the *Lama's* deck had dyed Storrs' white tunic and trousers as bright as themselves in their damp contact of the last four days, and now the sweat running in his clothes began to shine like varnish through the stain. I was so fascinated watching him that I never noticed the deepened brown of my khaki drill wherever it touched my body. He was wondering if the walk to the Consulate was long enough to wet me a decent, solid, harmonious colour; and I was wondering if all he ever sat on would grow scarlet as himself.~~

Inevitably, the losses were in wit and—literally, here—in narrative color, and the balance and pace of the text were adversely affected; yet T.E. was not at first seriously concerned, although this would be the version to reach the public —and the critics. His answers to queries from the publisher (Jonathan Cape), helpful in a lighthearted way, make this clear:

I attach a list of queries raised by F., who is reading the proofs. He finds these very clean, but full of inconsistencies in the spelling of proper names, a point which reviewers often take up. Will you annotate it in the margin, so that I can get the

Annotated: not very helpfully perhaps. Arabic names won't go into English, exactly, for their consonants are not the same as ours, and their vowels, like ours, vary from district to district. There are some "scientific systems" of transliteration, helpful to people who know enough Arabic not to need helping, but a wash-out proofs straightened?

for the world. I spell my names
anyhow, to show what rot the
systems are.

Slip 1. Jeddah and
Jidda used impartially
throughout. Intentional?

Rather!

Slip 16. Bir Wahei*da*,
was Bir Wahei*di*.

Why not? All one place.

Slip 20. Nuri, Emir of
the Ruwalla, belongs to the
"chief family of the Ruwalla."
On Slip 23 "Rualla horse,"
and Slip 38, "killed one
Rueli." In all later
slips "Rualla."

Should have also used Ruwala
and Ruala.

Slip 28. The Bisaita is
also spelt Biseita.

Good.

Slip 47. Jedha, the she-
camel, was Jedhah on Slip
40.

She was a splendid beast.

Slip 53. "Meleager, the
immoral poet." I have put
in "immortal" poet, but the
author may have meant immoral
after all.

Immorality I know. Immortality
I cannot judge. As you please:
Meleager will not sue us for
libel.

Slip 65. Author is
addressed "Ya Auruns,"
but on Slip 56 was "Aurans."

Also Lurens and Runs: not to
mention "Shaw." More to follow,
if time permits.

Slip 78. Sherif Abd el
Mayin of Slip 68 becomes
el Main, el Mayein, el
Muein, el Mayin, and el
Muyein.

Good egg. I call this
really ingenious.

While plans went ahead for serializing part of the abridgment in the *Daily Telegraph* and for publication immediately

thereafter, the private version made its very public appearance. November, 1926, was the month for its distribution—complete, sumptuously bound, and prefaced by a soon-controversial dedicatory poem.* *Seven Pillars* came in two varieties: the subscription copies, complete in number (although variant in order) of plates; and the incomplete copies (missing some or most plates), which were given to comparatively impecunious friends who had served with Lawrence in Arabia or to others in acknowledgment of services rendered. The 280,000-word production had cost thirteen thousand pounds. Reproducing the plates alone had cost more than all the subscription income had brought in. "The *Seven Pillars*," he reported in a note to subscribers, a pamphlet dated April, 1927, "was so printed and so assembled that nobody but myself knew how many copies were produced. I propose to keep this knowledge to myself. . . . I gave away, not perhaps as many copies as I owed, but as many as my bankers could afford, to those who had shared with me in the Arab effort, or in the actual production of the volume."

At last reinstated in the R.A.F., Lawrence was en route to India early in 1927 when, with the *Seven Pillars* distributed, the popular abridgment was released. The ensuing publicity delighted the author, but it would have embarrassed him had he been in England. Sales of *Revolt in the Desert* were brisk, over forty thousand copies in the first three weeks.† The re-

---

* See Chapter VI below.

† Lawrence had calculated that a sale of thirty thousand copies would pay off the debts he had incurred in the private edition, after which he would exercise his contractual right to withdraw the book. By June he had so instructed Cape, who by then had ninety thousand in print and had increased the firm's profits 150 per cent over the previous year. T.E.'s surplus royalties went to a charitable

views—although they dealt with a truncated shadow of the actual book whose author had taken it less seriously than he should have—treated *Revolt in the Desert* as if it were the already-legendary original *Seven Pillars*, which few of the critics had seen but of which none of them could have been unaware. Still, notices were generally laudatory, though (in the nature of all reviews) they often contradicted each other. Lawrence compiled a sampling of contradictions from cuttings forwarded by Charlotte Shaw, and sent selections to his friends:

Obscure, to the point of affectation.—*Tatler*

Effortless, artless-seeming, adequate prose.—Gerald Bullett

Has none of Doughty's biblical or Elizabethan anachronisms.
—John Buchan, *Saturday Review*

So imitative of Doughty as to be near parody.—Leonard Woolf, *Nation*

Writing as easy, confident and unselfconscious as a duck's swimming.
—*Literary Digest*

Gnarled texture twisted with queer adjectives and adverbs.
—Leonard Woolf

A scholar's style, simple, direct, free from ornament.
—H. W. Nevinson, Manchester *Guardian*

Positively breezy.—Bernard Shaw, *Spectator*

A cool, distinguished prose.—Eric Sutton, *Outlook*

Style here and there affectedly abrupt and strenuous, but mostly without affectation.—Edward Shanks

The style is like music.—C. F. G. Masterman

Style has a straightforward pierceness [*sic*], an intrepid directness.
—Ellis Roberts

---

trust he had set up for the welfare of R.A.F. families. The trust earned seventeen thousand pounds. The Cape firm earned about twenty-six thousand and moved to a new building at 30 Bedford Square.

When friends praised his style T.E. warmly shrugged it off. William Rothenstein was "over-kind," wrote Lawrence on May 5, 1927, adding a shrewd self-analysis. "I don't think much of it. My style is a made-up thing, very thickly encrusted with what seemed to me the tit-bits and clever wheezes of established authors. So, for book-learned people, threading it constantly, but not too sharply, [it] tickles their literary memory, by half-reminding them of half-forgotten pleasures. There isn't any good, or permanence, in such a derivative effort." Praise of his style, if it came from the wrong person, irritated Lawrence. In *Three Persons*, a book written while T.E. was in India, Andrew MacPhail praised the book as literature and condemned it as history. "What does he know about prose that he dare praise mine?" Lawrence complained. MacPhail's comments, however, are representative of the favorable contemporary consensus:

Nor is it what Lawrence saw in the desert that gives value to this book; it is what he thought of the things he saw. They passed through his mind. The desert and all that it contains have been described a hundred times, but never so delicately or with so sure a touch. He describes not things themselves, but the inner meaning and beauty that lie in them. The midday heat; the blaze of sun on basalt, rock or sand; the abomination of desolation; the pain of body; the glare from shining mud; the blackness of night and the brilliancy of stars; the cold snow; the small grass that comes in a green shimmer after rain; the rich herbage along the rivulets—anyone may see these, but Lawrence saw them through different eyes, through the eyes of a patriarch or prophetic Arab, and in detail, as one might say through the eyes of a camel. Any man may walk in the woods; it is given to few to see what Orlando saw in the Forest of Arden.

Writing to Edward Garnett, Lawrence confessed his annoyance at a review of his book by Herbert Read, who denigrated his style, accusing him of "ruthlessly cutting his text to suit his page." The cutting (from the Oxford to the subscription editions), T.E. insisted, was always based on how to better the prose, and most persons had told him that they thought the later version was superior to the earlier. Also, he pointed out, in reference to carping about the text as subservient to the format, there were many cases where the initial letter was not in the top left-hand corner of the page. He claimed he was "careful, exact, ambitious; and a hopeless failure because his aim was so high"; he was guilty of "over-thinking and overtrying" rather than indulging in "Max Beer-bohmish little perfections."[5] Max had much the same opinion of Lawrence and told S. N. Behrman that the "mixture of genius and insanity was too heady for him to do more than sample it."[6] (About Lawrence's later translation of the *Odyssey* Max once quipped to a friend, "I would rather not have been that translator than have driven the Turks from Arabia.")

A few diehards insisted that the Oxford version was superior to both the Subscription Edition and *Revolt in the Desert*. It was a conclusion which implied the special knowledge (and special favor) of having read the rare, semisecret Oxford text and was as much an announcement of having been "let in" as it was literary criticism. The earlier version still retains advocates, because of its more complete, ur-text quality and the comfortable feeling that no Procrustean games were played with its vocabulary and sentence structure.

With publication and criticism Lawrence suddenly shrank from relating his work to the epical mode, especially after Read's review of the book. "Isn't he ridiculous in seeking to measure my day-to-day chronicle by the epic standard?"

47

Lawrence wrote Garnett, overstating his case. "I never called it an epic, or thought of it as an epic, nor did anyone else to my knowledge. The thing follows an exact diary sequence, and it is literally true throughout." Although the book proceeded chronologically and remained reasonably close to the facts, the claims of exactitude and literal truth were overdoing the protest—and later T.E. referred to *Seven Pillars* with less diffidence as "an introspective epic." While it was true that Lawrence had scrupulously followed no one epical model, *Seven Pillars*, probably the only twentieth-century work to make epical figures out of contemporaries, may have been consciously patterned after a work of fiction—*Moby-Dick*, which "perhaps of all writings was the one closest in spirit to *Seven Pillars.*"[7] During the preparation of *Seven Pillars*, when Lawrence repeatedly praised *Moby-Dick*, he may have been suggesting not only a standard toward which he aspired but the structure for which he aimed in his own attempt at an epic. Melville's work had size, grandeur, and a quest for the absolute, all of which Lawrence admired unreservedly. And in Melville's combination of documentary with fictional approaches to an epical struggle, Lawrence could have discovered his method.

In a letter to Edward Garnett on August 28, 1922, T.E. described his own work in terms that again had intimations of Melville, for T.E. "looked on *Seven Pillars* as, in essence, tragedy—a victory in which no man could take delight." Then he asked, "Do you remember my telling you once that I collected a shelf of 'Titanic' books (those distinguished by greatness of spirit, 'sublimity' as Longinus would call it): and that they were *The Karamazovs, Zarathustra*, and *Moby Dick*? Well, my ambition was to make an English fourth. You will observe that modesty comes out more in the performance than in the aim!'"

T.E. remained consistent in his feeling that *Moby-Dick* was "a titan of a book," on occasion adding to the list of "big books" such other works as *War and Peace*, *Gargantua and Pantagruel*, *Don Quixote*, and *Leaves of Grass*.[8] There was always a special place for *Moby-Dick*, and a comparison of Melville's novel with *Seven Pillars* suggests that whatever Lawrence's other models (including Doughty's *Arabia Deserta*), there is a striking similarity in how both writers put their books together. In each case—whether the book is fiction, or fact embroidered and used fictionally—the quest of the protagonist is interleaved with documentary chapters. Lawrence gave background and dimension to his own first-person narrative with such interleaved chapters as one he described as "Arabia and the Arabs—emigrations, immigrations, and the current of tribal movements—sessile or nomad." Melville described the settling of Nantucket and the movement of Nantucketers from the island in whaling ships, taking to the sea for a livelihood the way Lawrence's Bedouin took to the sand. Similarly, other chapters of *Moby-Dick* fit into a documentary frame of reference. Melville discusses the history and geography of whaling, the migratory habits of whales, the anatomy of whales. The sternly factual enumeration of data, the cataloging of explicit details, is in the tradition of the classical epic, yet it provides form for Melville's treatises on cetology as for Lawrence's on Near Eastern history and sociology.

Other echoes of *Moby-Dick* reverberate through *Seven Pillars*. The formal, heightened language, sprinkled with notes of horror ("the peeled white body of the beheaded whale flashes like a marble sepulchre"); the accent on "the evil of my tale" (this from the opening sentence of *Seven Pillars*); the emphasis upon the brutish natural forces that thwart or warp the hopes and lives of men: these qualities in both works emphasize the beauty and terror in man's struggle for survival in an alien environment, whether it be ocean or desert. Lawrence need not be Melville's narrator Ishmael for the relevance of *Moby-Dick* to ring through the *Seven Pillars*; the primary impact appears to be one of structure, although Lawrence does not sustain his documentary interleaving to the very end. The concept had its usefulness. When he no longer needed it, he resumed his narrative.

Of Lawrence's literary friends, only E. M. Forster identified the *Moby-Dick* aspect of *Seven Pillars*, observing in a review of the posthumous trade edition that it was a *Moby-Dick* of a book, for Melville's masterpiece was ostensibly about catching a whale, and "round this tent-pole of a military chronicle T.E. has hung an unexampled fabric of portraits, descriptions, philosophies, emotions, adventures, dreams." That it was unexampled, however, Forster had himself disproven in his analogy, for his point was in the analogy itself.*

Even in its use of the journal or personal chronicle form, the sprawling *Seven Pillars* retains links with both *Moby-Dick* and classical narratives. Melville's first-person narrative is even less strict in its juxtaposition of chronology and docu-

---

* Jeffrey Meyers, discussing *Seven Pillars* in terms of Lawrence's aspiration to have his book stand beside *The Brothers Karamazov*, *Thus Spake Zarathustra*, and *Moby-Dick*, "to make an English fourth," sees Lawrence's achievements as "of the order, if not the genius, of these works, for it shares their epic and idealistic grandeur and portrays Melville's exalted quest for the absolute with Dostoevski's recondite and infernal soul states." [Jeffrey Meyers, "Nietzsche and T. E. Lawrence," *Midway* (Summer, 1970) revised slightly in Meyers' *The Wounded Spirit* (London, 1973).]

mentary than Lawrence's. "There are some enterprises," Melville's Ishmael explains, "in which a careful disorderliness is the true method."

One contemporary classicist sees in this "diary" form of *Seven Pillars* (by which description Lawrence played down his art) some comparison with Xenophon's *Anabasis*, Caesar's *Commentaries*, and Doughty's *Travels in Arabia Deserta*, "all favorites with Lawrence." Further, he suggests:

> Its archaic style has been misunderstood by some critics. Lawrence could write as contemporary English as any, and this is shown in *The Mint*. He deliberately chose a style . . . to enhance the outmoded epic gesture of his theme. He stops the flow of narrative with pages or even chapters of Thucydidean analysis of motives, [and] portraiture of the *dramatis personae*. It [*Seven Pillars*] includes a Platonic analysis of strategy as *episteme* (knowledge) versus *doxa* (appearance or opinion). Some of these take the form of prose choral odes of a tragedy which comment on the previous episode or actions. It is Herodotean in its digressions, again another favorite author of Lawrence.[9]

Bernard Shaw's review of *Revolt in the Desert*, a book which happened to be an abridgment of one which he had helped rewrite, appeared in the *Spectator* on March 12, 1927 (and was reprinted in the New York *Evening Post Literary Review* on April 16, 1927). Although Shaw had opposed the abridgment, he now found reason to applaud it:

> This abridgement of the famous Seven Pillars (itself an abridgement) contains as much of the immense original as anyone but an Imam has time to read. It is very handsomely and readably printed, and has not a dull or empty sentence from end to end. . . . Colonel Lawrence . . . can re-create any scene, any person, any action by simple description, with a vividness that leaves us in more complete possession of it than could the sensible and true avouch of our own eyes. He packs his narrative with detail that would escape nine hundred and ninety-nine out of a thousand observers. . . . And the descriptions are not interpolated: they are so woven into the texture of

the narrative, that the sense of the track underfoot, the mountains ahead and around, the vicissitudes of the weather, the night, the dawn, the sunset and the meridian, never leaves you for a moment.

You feel, too, the characters of the men about you: you hear the inflections of their voices, the changes in their expression, all without an instant of reader's drudgery. There is a magical brilliance about it; so that you see it at once with the conviction of reality and with the enchantment of an opera. Auda after his roaring camel charge, with his horse killed, his field glass shattered, and six bullet holes through his clothes, unhurt and ascribing his escape (under Allah) to an eighteen-penny Glasgow Koran which he had bought as a talisman for a hundred and twenty pounds, is at once a squalidly realistic Arab chieftain and a splendid leading baritone. The description has the quality of orchestration.

These blazing climaxes of adventure stand out from an inferno of tormented bodies and uneasy souls in which one is glad to meet a rascal for the sake of laughing at him. The subjective side which gives Miltonic gloom and grandeur to certain chapters of The Seven Pillars, and of the seventy and seven pillars out of which they were hewn, plays no great part in this abridgement. Lawrence's troublesome conscience and agonizing soul give place to his impish humor and his scandalous audacities; but it will interest the latest French school of drama to know that their effect remains, and imparts an otherwise unattainable quality to the work, even though they are not expressed.

Because of its size and bulk, the full text of *Seven Pillars of Wisdom* has been more discussed than read. It is an erratic book (T. E.'s cavalier attitude toward proper names extended to other things, too, such as dates), overpopulated by adjectives, often straining for effects and for "art." A reviewer of Shaw's *The Apple Cart* once complained (summing up a school of criticism of Shaw's dramaturgy) that the hero of the play was really the brain of Bernard Shaw, endlessly ratiocinating, its many cerebral facets sparkling like a diamond in the center of the stage. V. S. Pritchett, writing about *Seven Pillars* a quarter-century after its publication, similarly thought he saw in it "the will at work, hour by hour. Throughout a masterly narrative, packed with action, character and personal emotion, we have the extraordinary spectacle of a brain working the whole time. It is as if we could see the whole campaign thought by thought. The close texture of genius in action has rarely been so vividly done by an active man; it has been left, as a rule, to the self-watching invalids."[10] In a way, the work was also that of a "self-watching invalid," for, as Richard Aldington observed, "the book imposes on its readers the . . . strain of watching the author's painful mental and spiritual contortions as he suffered the onslaught of a severe nervous breakdown," a collapse "brought to consciousness" by the "hardships, responsibilities and dangers" of Arab rebellion.

The mannered prose, Aldington also pointed out, is not the pseudo-Elizabethan of Doughty, though the diffuse structure of *Seven Pillars* may be Doughtyesque. Lawrence "was aware of the drawbacks to Doughty's style" and Doughty's use "of hundreds of Arab words which have perfectly good English equivalents. Lawrence's dictum: 'Camel is a better word than thelul,' should be obeyed by all writers tempted into verbal local colour."[11]

The basic question which must be asked about *Seven Pillars of Wisdom* as a work of literature is whether it would still be read if the author were not the near-mythic "Lawrence of Arabia." Yet the question is unanswerable, for the man cannot be separated from his work, and the best of the uneven parts of *Seven Pillars* rise from superior journalism to high art. "Certain sections," Clifton Fadiman wrote soon after the book's posthumous publication, "are superb—the opening chapters analyzing the social, racial, and geographic bases of Arab character; the descriptions of Bedouin life and desert landscape, the scattered generalizations of strategy; the terrible scene in which Lawrence, refusing to surrender his chastity to a Turkish officer, is tortured until his spirit, no less than his body, is broken; the scattered reflections, acrid and ironic, on the shortcomings of the military mind; and the Hamlet soliloquies on the hopeless complexity of his own. For these things Lawrence will live as a writer." [12] Fadiman might have equally noted other scenes and other portraits, including the defeat-in-victory in Damascus.

Most of the criticism of *Seven Pillars* has concerned itself with its synthesis of man-of-action and man-of-letters, creating a critical psychology which will usually preclude a narrowly literary approach to the work. It is difficult, also, to separate the artless from the artful in Lawrence's use of the confessional mode. That he lived much, if not most, of his introspective epic makes it seem almost coincidental, for example, that he was reading Conrad's *Lord Jim* at about the time he was writing *Seven Pillars*, for the life of the Byronic, guilt-ridden, white-rajah hero bears an uncanny resemblance to that which Lawrence had already lived and largely recorded. The facts of the work's conception and development challenge a purely literary judgment. R. A. Scott-James would go further. The *Seven Pillars* to him is not merely the rare product of a man of action who was also by chance a man of letters: "The distinctive qualities which fitted him for literature were qualities without which he could not have succeeded in Arabia; and his literary ability needed, or appeared to need, important events shaped by himself for subject matter. He had an epic theme to handle; there would not have been this epic theme if he had not forced events to take that shape; and he produced the epic. His book is as full of heroes as the *Iliad*, and its Achilles is the author himself. What amazing egotism, one may be tempted to say, what colossal arrogance." Yet after some discussion of Lawrence's Doughty-inspired prose, Scott-James writes of the work's "muscular" language and "drama and splendour in the portraits of the chiefs," concluding that "The story has the distances of heroic legend, yet the closeness of autobiography."[13]

Whether or not a search for "distance" caused Lawrence to falsify or romanticize his Arabian experience, it is unquestionable that many events differ in details from the "facts" he reported in the *Arab Bulletin*, in his letters home or to friends, and in the accounts written by contemporaries on the scene. (Some of the reasons—literary, political, and psychological— have been noted earlier.) It is likely that studies of the discrepancies will continue to appear in reassessments of the *Seven Pillars*. The most interesting of these since Richard Aldington's venomous *Biographical Enquiry*, is Suleiman Mousa's *T. E. Lawrence: An Arab View* (1966), the first full-length study of Lawrence by an Arab to be published in English. Although Mousa's approach is different (he dislikes T.E. for playing down Arab abilities and achievements and for his alleged Zionist bias) his conclusions are similar, for any reconstruction of the "actual" events will bring to light names and deeds of Arab and Allied officers and troops who never appear in the index to *Seven Pillars*. Certainly Lawrence exaggerated and even invented some of the details in his narrative, but an analysis of these, rather than denigrating his achievement, only establishes his flair as a writer. One such episode picked apart by Mousa—and it is typical—is Lawrence's description of a raid on a Turkish train which took three pages in the *Arab Bulletin* for October 21, 1917, but thirty-two pages (and fourteen thousand words) in the Sub-scription Edition of *Seven Pillars*. In the later account T.E. wrote of having looked after "an ancient and very tremulous Arab dame" and assured her that she would not be harmed. Months later, he wrote, he received from Damascus "a letter and a pleasant little Baluchi carpet from lady Ayesha, daughter of Jellal el Lel, in memory of an odd meeting."

"I believe this to be a fabrication," Mousa declares, "and that the carpet was part of the booty plundered from the train. Lawrence may have fabricated the episode to forestall the charge that he shared with the bedouin this primitive custom of plundering the enemy." To prove his point—and there seems no question that it is proven—Mousa quotes a letter from Lawrence to a friend dated September 24, 1917, two days after his return from the raid. "The Turks . . . nearly cut us off as we looted the train," T.E. wrote, "and I lost some baggage, and nearly myself. My loot was a superfine red Baluchi prayer-rug."[14] Did Lawrence alter his story to protect himself from charges of looting? More likely the alteration of details was for literary reasons and as such was a successful touch. More of the same can be found on almost every page of *Seven Pillars*: it is Lawrence transmuting autobiographical chronicle into legend. It is the marrying of the "distance of heroic legend" with the "closeness of autobiography" that makes *Seven Pillars* (despite the technical flaws which close analysis of its text and texture may uncover) unique in literature.

Whether facts were falsified or magnified, invented or suppressed, belongs to history rather than to literature. Winston Churchill called the book "this treasure of English literature. As a narrative of war and adventure . . . it is unsurpassed. It ranks with the greatest books ever written in the English language. If Lawrence had never done anything except write this book as a mere work of the imagination his fame would last." It gleamed, thought Churchill, "with immortal fire." Throughout his life Churchill's estimation never changed. "Winston once told me," Lord Moran wrote, that "in his judgment [*Seven Pillars*] ranked with the greatest books ever written in the English language, with *The Pilgrim's Progress*, *Robinson Crusoe*, and *Gulliver's Travels*." Earlier Churchill himself had told Lawrence that.[15]

The combination of profound introspection and naked confession in *Seven Pillars*, wrote Jean Beraud Villars, reminded one of Proust or Gide. Villars found curious analogies between Lawrence and Gide, but a sentence like "I punished my flesh cheerfully, finding greater sensuality in the punishment than in the sin, so much was I intoxicated with pride at not sinning simply," he thought, could in tone and in manner have been ascribed to any one of the three. Lawrence's "balance between romanticism and naturalism," Villars wrote, "was the essence of a new form of literature" to be seized upon by a generation of writers who were reacting to an upbringing pervaded by naturalism yet unable to withstand its attractions. Lawrence, by combining romanticism with naturalism, gave new dignity to horror. It was a strangely mixed blessing, Villars implies, that

plucked at fibres that were not accustomed to vibrating. Into the *Seven Pillars* he dragged in the musty smells of homosexuality, of cruelty, and of death. A certain sadism which had been carefully expurgated from the accounts of the other war writers, who by tacit consent presented themselves as martyrs and paladins that were not supposed to have such troubled sensations.

Lawrence proved to be the forerunner. Before Malraux, the Koestler of

Darkness at Noon, Kafka and Jean-Paul Sartre, before the writers of the Resistance and those who described the Nazi and Soviet atrocities (without speaking of recent commercial novels, hybrid offsprings of brutality and pornography), he invented a style which was to be largely exploited by a whole generation of writers.[16]

The Lawrence style resisted extraction from mood: the "sickly conscience" was sardonically yet opulently exposed, and a world of beauty and brutality revealed. Soon after *Seven Pillars*, Malraux's terrorist Chan in *La Condition Humaine* (*Man's Fate*) would confess what Lawrence's sickly conscience had already made obvious: "A man who has never killed is a virgin."* It was, Jan Kott has written, "one of the most terrifying sentences written in the mid-twentieth century. . . . [It] means that killing is cognition, just as, according to the Old Testament, the sexual act is cognition; it also means that the experience of killing cannot be communicated, just as the experience of the sexual act cannot be conveyed. But this sentence means also that the act of killing changes the person who has performed it; from then on he is a different man living in a different world."[17] On both counts this was the Lawrence as revealed in the overwrought prose of *Seven Pillars of Wisdom*.

Richard Burton, Victorian translator of *The Arabian Nights* and a soldier often compared to Lawrence in personality as well as prose style, was never given to this kind of self-revela-

---

* Malraux has been greatly influenced by Lawrence, as Claude Mauriac has demonstrated explicitly in his *Malraux: Le Mal du Heros*, which is punctuated throughout by quotations from *Seven Pillars*. Malraux, however, never made himself his own hero. (His essay on *Seven Pillars*, published in three parts in *Liberte de l'Esprit* in April, May, and June, 1949, is not available in translation but is one of the most perceptive critiques of the work. A Malraux critique in English is the shorter "Lawrence and the Demon of the Absolute," in *Hudson Review*, Winter, 1956.)

tion. An examination of his *Pilgrimage to El-Medinah and Meccah*, written in Cairo and Bombay just after the experience, reveals much more detachment than does *Seven Pillars*.

Where Lawrence was soft and poetic, Burton was brisk and tough-minded; where Lawrence was introspective and selective, Burton displayed a veritable mania for fact-collecting. Both men wrote from notes and journals, but gave the impression of having the gift of total recall. Both were scholars as well as soldiers and adventurers, and talented at describing landscapes and people. But where Lawrence wrote a luminous self-portrait that greatly exposed himself, Burton successfully hid himself and exposed the whole Arab world.

When Lawrence wrote of the Arabs, "Pain was to them a solvent, a cathartic, almost a decoration, to be fairly worn while they survived it," one can be fairly certain, in the light of all that is known of him, that he was then writing of himself. Burton's generalizations were often equally sweeping, but much less projections of his own character, though when he wrote, "Travellers, like poets, are mostly an angry race," the direction of the arrow was unmistakable.[18]

Richard Aldington's iconoclastic *Biographical Enquiry* marveled that "a style so high-flown and exacting" could have been maintained "through so long a book" but accused the author of "verbal dodging," factual inexactitude, and an "unscrupulous" use of words (such as his "appeal to puritan prejudice of the word 'clean' "). The Aldington conclusion: "He might have written much better if he had not striven so painfully to write too well."

Herbert Read, on the other hand, found its matter inferior to its manner, partly because—like Aldington a veteran of the French trenches—he found no epic grandeur in a "straining after grace," or in a fringe adventure which was little more than "a dance of flies in the air" beside the agony of the western front. Willing, like others, to compare *Seven Pillars* with *Arabia Deserta*, he found the former the gross inferior.

Doughty filled him with wonder and reverence at every page—"a man who was a great mind, a great patriarch among men, a great enduring character, pensive but self-possessed, inquiring but full of certainty." For Read the key word was the last one, for he insisted narrowly that great books could only be written in "moods of spiritual light and intellectual certainty." In *Seven Pillars of Wisdom* he was "only conscious of an uneasy adventurer; of an Oxford graduate with a civilian and supercilious lack of the sense of discipline; of a mind, not great with thought, but tortured by some restless spirit that drives it out into the desert, to physical folly and self-immolation, a spirit that never triumphs over the body and never attains peace."[19] What Read was dismissing, it seems, was not so much Lawrence as the twentieth century.

A reappraisal of *Seven Pillars* by the irascible Malcolm Muggeridge made previous hostile criticism of Lawrence and his book seem timid, for Muggeridge complained of the "hollowness" and "total solemnity" of the prose; he felt the events described were "happenings too remote from reality for one to care whether they are true or false." Yet Muggeridge conceded Lawrence one insight. Though the campaign T.E. engineered in Arabia "proved historically and militarily insignificant . . . it provided a flickering afterglow of antique warfare which was going to be flattened out, and perhaps obliterated, by the totalitarian sort."[20] The perspective rejects *Seven Pillars* as literature only to rescue it as history or sociology, although E. M. Forster had earlier found both virtues in the work.

[Lawrence] also contributed to sociology, in recording what is probably the last of the picturesque wars. Camels, pennants, the blowing upof little railway trains by little charges of dynamite in the desert—it is unlikely to recur. Next time the aeroplane will blot out everything in an indifferent death, but the aeroplane in this yarn is only a visitor, which arrives in the last chapters to give special thrills. A personal note can still be struck. It is possible to pot [a shot] at the fat station master as he sits drinking coffee with his friends . . . good . . . got him . . . he rolls off his deck chair! Steal up behind the shepherds and score their feet, so that they do not carry the news! Hide under the bridge in the rain all night! This is not only agreeable to the reader, it is important to the historian. Because it was waged under archaistic conditions, the Arab revolt is likely to be remembered. It is the last effort of the war-god before he laid down his godhead and turned chemist.[21]

Again, although this was a man of letters speaking, he had a historian's insight into the work.* Its development, as the preceding chapter has demonstrated, was still from history to something else, having passed through stages which shifted its emphasis away from chronicle, even away from the outside events it nevertheless still narrated. As André Malraux analyzed it, "The only means the spirit has for escaping the absurd is to involve the rest of the world in it, to imagine it, to express it. Little by little the Revolt began to take second place while the main interest passed to the absurdity of life for a man reduced to solitude by an irreducible inner conflict and the meditation it imposed. . . . What actually separated him from the Revolt, what he wanted to express in order to make his book great, is that every human action is defiled by its own nature."[22] Going inside himself to evoke the "remorse of being one's self,"[23] Lawrence could not at the same time bend to a historian's scruples about facts, even if he began with them. "I must take up again my mantle of fraud in the East," he observed disarmingly in *Seven Pillars.* "With

---

* One historian, on the other hand, has dismissed the book as being without redeeming literary merit. "T. E. Lawrence," wrote A. J. P. Taylor crustily, "provided the upper classes with a substitute for literature."

my certain contempt for half measures I took it up quickly and wrapped myself in it completely. It might be fraud or it might be force: no one should say that I could not play it."

One of the problems raised by consideration of *Seven Pillars* as a major twentieth-century work of literature is that despite its confessed inexactitude and subjectivity it *is* a work of history—a work which has the poetry of history. G.B.S. seems to have hoped as he saw it in progress that it would become history on the Thucydidean model, where the events were brought to vivid life, however great the cost was in the loss of exactitude; but Lawrence's book of the Arabian revolt is only history as is the *Iliad* history. As *literature* it does not approach so great a work as the *Iliad* but rather has the inaccuracies, extravagances, diffuseness, artificiality—and sustained genius for language—of an epic in the Miltonic manner but misplaced in time: misplaced because in its frank subjectivity and its naturalism we see its peculiarly twentieth-century aspects.

Henri Montherlant in his *Threnody for the Dead of Verdun* talked of the war "nostalgia" of veteran soldiers and claimed that one could say that it had been, ironically, the most "tender" human experience of contemporary life. His countryman, the Jesuit Teilhard de Chardin, wrote that the most compelling fascination of the battlefield was that in action one discovered a lucidity not otherwise vouchsafed: "This heightening is not got without pain. All the same it is indeed a heightening. And that is why in spite of everything, one loves the front and regrets it."[24] The power of *Seven Pillars of Wisdom* lies not only in its mannered prose and its epical evocations but in its dramatizing such paradoxes.

On Lawrence's death nearly a decade after the release of the Subscription Edition, Jonathan Cape, considering T.E.'s embargo as effective only in his lifetime, quickly ordered a new printing of *Revolt in the Desert*. A. W. Lawrence, citing his brother's wishes, forbade it but agreed to license publication of a trade edition of *Seven Pillars*. The handsomely designed and illustrated edition was released within a mere two months of the agreement, on July 29, 1935. For the text the firm used a copy of the American-printed copyright text given to Cape by George Doran in 1926. But the new edition was not identical. There had been no Chapter xi in the original, for the renumbering to account for the excised Chapter 1 had only gone that far. The 1935 edition removed that anomaly. And there were lines cut to avoid hurting living persons. Few readers knew or noticed. The book sold in the hundreds of thousands on both sides of the Atlantic, although at thirty shillings (in England) its price was four times that of a novel. *Seven Pillars* is still in print. The newest (1973) edition has restored the cuts—even the names.

CHAPTER III

The Mint

LATE in 1922, at the end of each long training day at the R.A.F. camp at Uxbridge, Lawrence would sit in bed, blankets pulled over drawn-up knees, and write letters to friends or scribble notes for *The Mint*. His method was outlined not only in letters to the Garnetts, to E. M. Forster, and to Charlotte Shaw, but in the work itself: "Day by day I had been putting down these notes on our Depot life, often writing in bed from roll-call till lights out, using any scrap of paper. So I seemed only to be writing letters. They were now grown to an unmanageable crumpled bulk. Yet I could not send the earlier ones away, for I often went back with fuller understanding to a past experience and implemented it; or ran the collected impressions of, say, three fire-pickets into one."

The book began with a picture of the frightened would-be recruit; he was scruffy, hungry, and worried about discovery —or refusal of enlistment—or both:

God, this is awful. Hesitating for two hours up and down a filthy street lips and hands and knees tremulously out of control, my heart pounding in fear of that little door through which I must go to join up. Try sitting a moment in the churchyard? That's caused it. The nearest lavatory, now. Oh yes, of course, under the church. . . . A penny; which leaves me fifteen. Buck up, old seat-wiper: can't tip you and I'm urgent. Won by a short head. My right toe is burst along the welt and my trousers are growing fringes. One reason that taught me I wasn't a man of action was this routine melting of the bowels before a crisis. However, now we end it. I'm going straight up and in. . . .

"Nerves like a rabbit." The Scotch-voiced doctor's hard fingers go hammer, hammer, hammer over the loud box of my ribs. I must be pretty hollow.

"Turn over: get up; stand under here: make yourself as tall as you can: he'll just do five foot six, Mac: chest—say 34. Expansion—by Jove, 38. That'll do. Now jump: higher: lift your right leg: hold it there: cough: all right: on your toes: arms straight in front of you: open your fingers wide: hold them so: turn round: bend over. Hullo, what the hell's those marks? Punishment?" "No Sir, more like persuasion Sir, I think." Face, neck, chest, getting hot.

"H . . . m . . . m . . ., that would account for the nerves." His voice sounds softer. "Don't put them down, Mac. Say *Two parallel scars on ribs.* What were they, boy?"

"Superficial wounds, Sir."

"Answer my question."

"A barbed-wire tear, over a fence."

"H . . . . m . . . m . . ."[1]

Lawrence's first enlistment—arranged through his friend at the air ministry, Sir Hugh Trenchard, the chief of the air staff—came to an abrupt halt when his thin disguise as "J. H. Ross" was exposed in headlines in London newspapers in December. The embarrassed air ministry released him early in 1923.

"I still feel miserable at the time I missed, because I was thrown out that first time," he wrote E. M. Forster afterwards. "I had meant to go on to a Squadron, & write the real Air Force, and make it a book—a BOOK, I mean. It is the

biggest subject I have ever seen, and I thought I could get it."
But his discharge broke the "rhythm" of his progress, and
after the creatively uninspiring blank of his tank corps years
(crowded by the preparation of *Seven Pillars*, and physical
and emotional misery) his air force reinstatement provided
him only with material to balance the bitterness and the
savagery of the earlier experience, "for fairness' sake." This
renewal of the journal would become its third section, one
built upon extracts from letters to his friends—primarily from
his letters to one of them.

The organization of *The Mint* was worked out in India.
Writing from the R.A.F. base at Karachi while revising and
augmenting his earlier material, Lawrence asked Charlotte
Shaw to mail back to him the Cranwell notes of 1925 and
1926 which he had left with her, yellow slips of paper describing a hoisting of the colors ceremony, guard inspection, and
his comments on a chaplain's sermon on the death of Queen
Alexandra, the widow of Edward vii. The "final" version of
the book he had begun in 1922 would be the assembling of his
rewritten notes on his first R.A.F. experience ("Raw Material" and "In the Mill") with his happier life at Cranwell
("Service"). In a preface to the third section he stressed
"how different, how humane" life could be under a benign
regimen, an experience already suffused with nostalgia for
him from the perspective of India. "There is no continuity in
these last pages," he wrote, "—and a painful inadequacy: but
perhaps some glint of our contentment may shine from between my phrases into your eyes."

In a final sentence, given a paragraph to itself, he added,
"How can any man describe his happiness?" It was an ironic
bliss when, with a million and a half men unemployed in

England, enlistment meant the open acknowledgment of defeat by life.

On January 4, 1928, he mailed Charlotte the first twenty thousand words of his condensed Uxbridge chronicle. The manuscript was intended less for Charlotte than for Shaw's critical eye: "If G.B.S. sees any of the chapters & says anything related to them, will you tell it [to] me, uncensored?" In a cynical reference to the critics of *Seven Pillars*, he added, "There will be no reviews of this book, to fail to tell me anything about myself as a writer. I fancy it better, in shape and strength, to the war-book: but I confess I do not see in either of them more than the psychological interest of souls in travail."[2]

It was more than three months before the rest of *The Mint*, in a version Lawrence transcribed on his R.A.F. office typewriter, was mailed. It was less than seventy thousand words —shorter than his earlier handwritten draft.

In its near-final form Lawrence's book followed the pattern of recruit training, but it amalgamated similar incidents taken from notes and letters into a single, more emphatic—and sometimes more hysterical—experience. He had reduced the fifty names in his notes to fifteen, both to avoid confusion and to protect himself in some places from too obvious identification. He tried to balance his scenes of contentment with air force life and his scenes of splenetic rage at the desecration of a recruit's essential inviolate humanity. He described dehumanization as an ironic good, but revealed the service's means toward that end—the metaphor of minting conveying the idea (as he wrote Air Marshal Trenchard early in 1928) of men being stamped into the R.A.F.'s image of what the man in the ranks should be, "violently stamping an indelible mark on coarse material"—the molding "of a soldier's body and soul into a uniform pattern," as Villars describes it. But Villars does not mention the subtle reverberations of the title of the French translation, which T.E. might have appreciated. *La Matrice* can mean matrix, or die mold—or womb.

Lawrence also aimed at what he called the "feel" of a camp for recruit training, balanced by the "feel" of service at an R.A.F. station. The complex of balances was worked out in short, journal-entry chapters: the lyrical ("landscape passages," he called them) opposed to the oppressive and the humdrum; the sentimental opposed to the stark and the obscene. As G.B.S. later told him, *The Mint*, in seeking that balance, wobbled between a document for the files* and an artistic work. In Zolaesque naturalism (with some lapses into fine writing), which T.E. probably thought to be much closer to Swiftian satire than to Zola, Lawrence had evoked the barracks and its inhabitants while—through the act of setting it down on paper—exorcising some of his morbid urge to brutalize and humiliate himself.

G.B.S. was frank about *The Mint* to Lawrence. He bluntly suggested a rewriting to add the humor in barracks life that

---

* T.E. rejected one opportunity to write the R.A.F. story literally from the files as well as for history. In 1924, while he longed for reinstatement in the air force, the R.A.F. was searching for an author to write its young history. Trenchard suggested that the supplicant could reenter the R.A.F. as its official—and officer-rank—historian. "I thought for a night and then declined," Lawrence wrote his friend D. G. Hogarth. "The job is a hazardous one (T. wants a 'literary' history, the C.I.D. a 'technical'), attractive, very, to me by reason of its subject. The terms (three years) compare unfavorably with the six which the army offers; and the responsibility is one which I'd regret as soon as I shouldered it." In a letter to Trenchard, Lawrence declined, and vowed to remain in the army until he could reenter the air force on the "ground floor." It took him, even after much political intervention on the part of his friends, an additional two years to change his status from "Private Shaw" to "Aircraftman Shaw," but he had his way, and persisted in writing his own air force book.

T.E. had deliberately ignored but which was necessary to make the work readable, and the scrapping of the gratuitous bad taste which he saw as precluding the book's publication for a mass audience. (That Lawrence's literary impulse did not necessarily extend to trade publication of what he had felt compelled to write was something G.B.S. found difficult to comprehend.) *The Mint* was, Shaw declared, a work of genuine literary power, as well as of documentary value for the experience it recorded. Any kind of reticence was wrong. Even if only a bowdlerized version could be published, the original should be preserved as a document.

From the literary standpoint Shaw confined his suggestions for cuts to two substantial passages in the manuscript, both from later parts of the manuscript. "Police Duty" (Part III, Chapter 12) was a retelling of a military policeman's morbid story of a London incident in which a tart concealed her dead infant in her bed while entertaining a corporal on her couch. Perhaps remembering that T.E. more easily accepted criticism based upon literary considerations, G.B.S. condemned the tale not as an example of bad taste but as a tissue of purple-patchy descriptive passages which read, he contended, like a student effort. "Funeral" (Part III, Chapter 9), which G.B.S. also suggested scrapping, described a church parade to which Lawrence and his comrades were subjected (including a long sermon on Queen Alexandra's reputation for beauty and virtue) on the day the queen was buried. Furious at what he considered to be folly and imposition even in good weather, let alone on a morning of chilly autumn fog (earlier, the troops had to stand at attention while the drums rolled and rolled, and the flag agonizingly crept down to half-mast),

T.E. recalled his final memory of the aged widow of Edward VII, mummified-looking in her last, pitiful years:

There had to be parade service the day she was buried. Our distrusted chaplain preached one of his questionable sermons. He spoke of the dead Queen as a Saint, a Paragon: not as an unfortunate, a long-suffering doll. With luscious mouth he enlarged upon her beauty, the beauty which God, in a marvel of loving-kindness, had let her keep until her dying.

My thoughts fled back sharply to Marlborough House. The yellow, scaling portal: the white-haired footmen and doorkeepers, whiter than the powder of their hair: the hushed great barn-like halls: the deep carpet in which our feet dragged unwillingly to the ceiling-high fireplace which dwarfed the whispering Miss Knollys and Sir Dighton. She incredibly old, wasted, sallow: he a once huge man, whose palsied neck had let down the great head on the breast, where its gaping mouth wagged almost unseen and unheard in the thicket of beard which overgrew the waistcoat. . . he was so old, and Miss Knollys so old that this seemed a cruel duty which kept them always on their feet. . . .

We had to wait, of course: that is the prerogative of Queens. When we reached the presence, and I saw the mummied thing, the bird-like head cocked on one side, not artfully but by disease, the red-rimmed eyes, the enamelled face, which the famous smile scissored across all angular and heart-rending:—when I nearly ran away in pity. The body should not be kept alive after the lamp of sense has gone out. There were the ghosts of all her lovely airs, and little graces, the once-effective sways and movement of the figure which had been her consolation. Her bony fingers, clashing in the tunnel of their rings, fiddled with albums, penholders, photographs, toys upon the table: and the heart-rending appeal played on us like a hose, more and more terribly.[3]

The Alexandra passages were in bad taste, Shaw warned, and it was unnecessarily cruel, savage, and ignoble to so write of the infirmities of senility—which required instead man's most humane understanding.[4]

Since *The Mint* was not published in Lawrence's lifetime, there is no way of knowing whether these sweeping suggestions would ever have been carried out. That such changes were doubtful is indicated by the revisions T.E. began making in his last years, and the favorable earlier reception of some of the passages objected to by G. B. S. by such friends as Siegfried Sassoon, who thought the Queen Alexandra section was "wonderful," and E. M. Forster, who called the Queen Alexandra piece "brilliant." T.E. retained the passages, making only minor alterations.

Other comments by both Charlotte and G.B.S. pleased T.E. more, for both thought the book generally spare and severe—an appropriate parallel to the service uniform and the barracks room, T.E. believed. The patches of overwriting annoyed Shaw, who labeled them "Literary Lawrence" and suggested as title for one chapter that he thought reeked of the lamp, "Literary to the Last." He worried over the high adjective count, and the surviving manuscript shows stylistic changes in Shaw's hand—mainly his making T.E.'s diction more precise. For example, "stay put for ages" became "stay put indefinitely."[5] While T.E. accepted mechanical changes, he objected to Shaw's idea that the book had to be either a "record of fact" or a "work of art." *The Mint*, he thought, was the better for being neither. It was his effort to succeed where he had convinced himself he had failed in *Seven Pillars*—"to make history an imaginative thing," to "try at dramatizing reality." His understanding of his earlier failure, he insisted, had made him a writer—not the fact of the work itself.

From India Lawrence considered *The Mint* itself the inevitable act of the writer he had become; but publication would be an "indulgence." Having the typescript circulate among his friends was sufficient satisfaction. Unlike the earlier book, *The Mint* was personal, not an episode in history, like the *Seven Pillars*, "which had to be put on record." He had no intention of writing another book *for publication* at the time, although he clearly had no intention of ceasing writing. The volume of his letter-writing, for example, remained enormous, at severe cost, in postage, to his ability to supply his other needs. Before he published again under his own name, he reflected, he would have to become "a different character"—perhaps a reference to the civilian status he knew he would have to resume in 1935.

One thing *The Mint* enabled Lawrence again to do was to luxuriate in close criticism of his work by those whom he thought his literary betters. The very fact of the criticism remaining private and personal appealed to his ego while it did not threaten the nagging sense of inferiority as a writer which he may have feared publication would expose. As a result the volume of *Letters to T. E. Lawrence* is packed with close critiques—mostly diplomatically favorable—of *The Mint* as well as of *Seven Pillars*: letters from John Buchan, Winston Churchill, Noel Coward, Edward Garnett, E. M. Forster, Augustus John, Rudyard Kipling, H. G. Wells, Bernard Shaw, and others. T.E. was exhilarated not so much by praise as by the close attention creative people were willing to pay to his texts. Shaw's literary criticism of *The Mint*, he told G.B.S., was "much more exciting" than the playwright's entreaties to publish the work, and he luxuriated in responding to such criticism.

You put your finger on two of the three or four inventions in the book: first the purple night-scape in the story of the dead infant. What Corporal Williams said was: "Christ, it was as black as hell." I found that in my notes, and copied it. When I read it, stark on paper, here in Karachi, the whole story felt true. So I pulled out his too-likely phrase, and piled black Pelion on Ossa, to shake the scene out of fact into Dunsanity. Overdid it, of course, as usual. Now I'll write and tell Garnett to cross out the purple lines, and restore the bald reality.

The other passage about Queen Alexandra, shows that I've wholly missed my target with you. As I worked on it I was trying to feel intensely sorry for the poor old creature who had been artfully kept alive too long. I was trying to make myself (and anyone else who read it) shake at the horrible onset of age. And you find a touch of the grinning street-arab. Mrs. Shaw found it cruel. I was saying to myself "*You*'ll be like that, too, unless you die sooner than the Queen . . . " but it wasn't personal.[6]

The same day Lawrence mailed a long letter to Edward Garnett, acknowledging that much of it was an extract from a letter to G.B.S., and suggesting that Garnett line out the purple passages in the chapter on Queen Alexandra. Much of the Cranwell section, he admitted, came from private letters to Mrs. Shaw he had borrowed.

Later Lawrence wrote to E. M. Forster to thank him for a letter in praise of *The Mint* (a letter he confessed having read eight times and was going to read again) and admitted that *The Mint*'s private reception had not been all of the encomium variety. In particular, the chapter on Queen Alexandra's funeral had had a mixed reception: "Garnett praises that. Shaw says it's the meanness of a guttersnipe laughing at old age. I was so sorry and sad at the poor old queen." Forster had called the section on Alexandra "brilliant," pressed T.E. as to why he shouldn't "write all sorts of books," and added —a curious suggestion, given his own homosexuality, then unspoken but understood in his circle—"I hadn't, before, known whether you could use many kinds of experience, or whether—as far as creation was concerned—you would stop at Arabia. I rather wish you would make yourself examine

and describe women: many of them are about, and reluctance* can lead us to profitable discoveries." Candidly, T. E.
estimated in return that he had a "cherrystone talent," and
besides felt literarily "as dry as a squeezed orange."[7] It was a
difficult confession for one whose ambition to write was even
greater than his desire to be read.

Edward Garnett passed T.E.'s typescript on to his son
David, who also gratified "Shaw" with a critique. "Like the
Seven Pillars," the younger Garnett suggested, "the book is
half record of fact, half spiritual experience: my father did
well to compare it with Dostoevsky's House of the Dead.
Your experience was far worse than his: convicts do not enlist
for prison; they do not pretend willingly to give up being men
in order to become a chain-gang." But after the encomiums
came the guarded criticism: "I mean there is a tendency for
you to regard all sort of incidents as illuminating & valuable
which are neither. . . . There is a flavour of 1915 (a flavour of
Rupert [Brooke]'s sonnets!). To me this gives a touch of insanity such as I always feel in reading of—battles—wars—
religious revivals & similar aberrations of humanity." But,
David Garnett concluded, *The Mint* was valuable not because a well-known personality had written it, but because it
was "finely written." And it was important not because, as
T.E. insisted, it was about the birth-pangs of the military
service of the future, but because it was "an account of the
prolonged torture of the individual & his heroic but incomplete resistance to the torture. He even preserves detachment
while it is going on. There are some subjects which are too

* The word *reluctance* seems wrong in the context but it is so transcribed in
David Garnett (ed.), *Letters to T. E. Lawrence.*

narrow & too painful to lend themselves to an artist. The tortures of the damned, & the temptations of the saints. But the Mint succeeds where all such fail." In a revealing phrase, Garnett noted that T.E. had become in his two books an artist "who chooses pain for his subject." T.E. at first either failed, or was unwilling, to understand. He had received from Garnett, he wrote E. M. Forster, a "most queer letter about The Mint." Before long he understood, and he snatched at Garnett's meaning. If *Seven Pillars* was, as subtitled, a triumph, Garnett had written, *The Mint* was an agony. "You have it in one word," Lawrence wrote back. "I should have written *an agony* after the Title."[8] Afterwards, when he wrote to Jonathan Cape, publisher of his earlier book, he referred to "*The Mint*, an agony of the Royal Air Force."

Later, Siegfried Sassoon, once a war poet like Rupert Brooke, offered his own speculation about *The Mint* to T.E. "Your book is a drama of mind versus body—isn't it? You resent 'coddling' your body, & resent the d——d apparatus altogether. . . . Your book has also reminded me rudely of the gross brutality of 'unprotected' human existence. How can one go on writing lyrics in the presence of physical facts, (such as age, ache, penury, & imprisonment, plus the faces one sees in the streets of London, & the conventions & false refinements of people one, if possible, avoids knowing)—?"[9]

Not everyone who saw *The Mint* in typescript saw it with T.E.'s authorization. Like *Seven Pillars* in its preliminary text, it had a history of surreptitious borrowings, for having read *The Mint* conferred on the reader a rare and sought-after distinction in literary society. Not everyone who read it found it praiseworthy or even palatable. Sholto Douglas (Lord Douglas of Kirtleside), then a high staff officer with the R.A.F., was one who read *The Mint* without T.E.'s knowledge, and whose reaction reflected more a military than a literary opinion. It was, he considered, "thoroughly poisonous" and dishonest:

It was understandable that a man of T. E. Lawrence's age and background should be unhappy as a recruit in the company of much younger men at the R.A.F. Depot at Uxbridge; and it was only to be expected that he should feel like a fish out of water. How could a man of his temperament and upbringing and experience and, to boot, an Oxford don of about thirty-five years of age and a former Colonel in the Army, feel otherwise? He was masquerading as a raw recruit in the Air Force, and naturally the routine and the physical training and the drill and the coarseness of the life were distasteful to him. But he had deliberately chosen to live a life designed not for a highly educated man who was approaching middle age but for young men of nineteen or twenty years of age, many of whom were by no means bright and were certainly not well-educated, and most of whom were straight from civil life.

The way in which T. E. Lawrence wrote about the R.A.F. . . . in *The Mint* was mean enough in spirit; but what I found quite inexcusable was the spite and the vicious unfairness of what he had to say about [Bonham-Carter] the Commandant of the Depot at that time. Lawrence made him out to be a brute and a sadist. I knew that officer well. . . . He had a good record in the First World War, in which he had been very severely wounded. He was a strict disciplinarian, but that was exactly the quality most needed in the Commandant at a Recruit Training Depot.*

In the long run, many of us came to feel that T. E. Lawrence, so far as the R.A.F. was concerned, was scarcely more than a nuisance. To appreciate that one has only to imagine the difficulties that he created for the

* "I was studying how to keep step with his dotting false leg when he swung round on me, and shouted to know why the bloody hell I'd let the point of my stick droop towards the ground. The rage-distorted face was thrust down into mine, making me sick at the near-squalor of those coarse hairs which bushed from his ears and nose, and the speckle of dark pits which tattooed his skin. . . . The Commandant liked men who cringed. . . . His character was compounded of the corruptions of courage, endurance, firmness and strength: he had no consideration . . . no mercy and no fellowship. . . . We felt that we should be more considered than our food and our clothes. He treated us like stock-cattle: so that the sight of him became a degradation to us." (*The Mint*, Part i, Chapter 20)

more junior officers under whom he served as an airman when they knew that he was writing personal letters direct to Air Vice-Marshal Sir Oliver Swann, the Air Member for Personnel, and to other senior and distinguished officers, and even to the Chief of the Air Staff, Trenchard himself.[10]

The chief of the air staff himself was more understanding but no less worried about the potential the book had for making trouble. In July, 1928, Trenchard wrote to Lawrence after having borrowed a typescript of *The Mint* (at T.E.'s suggestion) from Edward Garnett. "I read every word of it," he told Lawrence. "And I seemed to know what was coming each line, and I feel no soreness, no sadness, about your writing, and yet again I feel all of a tremble in case it gets out and into the hands of people who do not know life as it is." Lawrence assured Trenchard that it would not be published before 1950, if then; and their relationship remained as cordial as it could have been, given Lawrence's insistence upon remaining at the opposite pole in rank from that of his old friend. But Trenchard also saw to it that there was an air force file, No. S44G8, marked "Precautions for Preventing Publication of *The Mint*." No precautions ever had to be taken.[11]

To Jonathan Cape, T.E. explained that Trenchard was not the major factor in keeping the book from appearing in print: its author was.

It's not the sort of book to be decently published. Every character in it is real and every incident actually happened! That would be a new sort of note to put on a flyleaf.

Trenchard isn't the difficulty: at least only a minor one. I am the prime stumbling block. All the fellows in the hut are in the book: and they would regard the record of themselves as a betrayal of confidence. When that sort of man goes to be photographed he puts on what he calls his "best":— a special suit of clothes:—and they wouldn't relish the birthday suits in which I draw them. Nor would I like them to think that I've given them away: though I think I'm absolutely justified in doing so, and have done 'em honour. By 1950 there will be no reality or soreness left: and till then the book shall remain hidden:—unless your firm coughs up a million! Twenty-two years. I wonder if you'll retire before that?[12]

Wyndham Lewis afterwards wondered what the R.A.F. hierarchy had to fear in *The Mint*. It was, he wrote a friend, "a bawdy song or two, and thousands of soldiers' oaths, nothing more."[13] This carried denigration too far. In what remains the finest essay on Lawrence the writer, R. P. Blackmur (who at the time had been able to read the lone accessible American text, the copyright edition deposited in the Library of Congress) summed up *The Mint* as "in the first part, a record of animal debasement, and in the second much shorter [Cranwell] part the intimation of spiritual release through a disciplined and surrendered life. It is thus an essay in moral immolation and intellectual asceticism, religious in prompting, escapist in enactment; so that its final significance, while religious, is the significance of an irrational, restricted religion; which is to say that it is abnormal in the sense of being *merely* individual."[14]

Although G.B.S. wanted twenty copies of an unexpurgated version of *The Mint* printed for the record, all that Lawrence would agree to eventually was the production of a few extra typescripts for safekeeping. Later Doubleday—in 1935—printed a few copies from one of the typescripts to safeguard the American copyright but prohibitively priced the copies to keep the work, in effect, private.

Until the end of his life he continued re-revising the text in a typescript made from a Garnett copy, making small changes on each page and an occasional change which involved no more than chapter titles, capitalization, or punctuation. His plans were to print a limited edition of the book himself, on a handpress, once he was out of the service, and for a frontispiece illustration he had arranged with Emery Walker for sufficient reproductions of a drawing of himself in aircraftman uniform by Augustus John.[15] He never abandoned planning new touches for *The Mint*, toward its eventual publication, convinced it was his authentic claim to literary survival on his own merits and not on the accident of war. Perhaps for that reason he never felt satisfied that he had finished with the revising.

To E. M. Forster, Lawrence had written that he would not permit the book's publication while "the fellows with me in the force" would feel horror "at my giving them away. . . . So *The Mint* shall not be circulated before 1950." Arrangements for publication by Cape were made in 1947, but in 1950 the martinet officer about whom T.E. had written so viciously in Chapter xx was still alive. In 1955 *The Mint* was first released to the general public; and readers, expecting gross titillation after nearly three decades of rumor and secrecy had exaggerated the book's improprieties, were disappointed. Rather than appearing as a precursor* of such "black" satires as Miller's *Tropic of Cancer*, Céline's *Voyage au bout de la nuit*, and Durrell's *The Black Book*, *The Mint*, because of its generation-long delay in release and the intervening horror of another world war, became a contemporary, instead, of *The*

---

* *The Mint* may have had a precursor in a book Lawrence is known to have read, Henri Barbusse's *Le Feu* (1916), a vision of trench-warfare filled with soldiers' argot and physical terror; however *The Mint* in a crucial sense compounds the horror by transferring it to a peacetime, barracks situation.

Naked and the Dead and *From Here to Eternity*. Ironically, it thus became the embalmed document that G.B.S. had wanted preserved. Yet even in 1955 the trade edition timidly left white spaces where the limited edition printed the peppering of four-letter words, apparently following the traditional but since discredited publishing philosophy that only the wealthy could be trusted to react appropriately to obscenity. Current reprint editions print *all* the words.

With the perspective of years which makes Beckett's early fiction, Genet's transparent autobiographies, and Lawrence's *Mint* seem similarly distant, we can condone T.E.'s experiments in the surreal, the sadistic, and the grotesque without concluding that the whole must equal in power the sum of its parts. The violence of the satire no longer seems unreasonable in relation to the object satirized, for the peg upon which the satire hangs is less important than its success as symbol; and at least several of the episodes in *The Mint* reach a tragic —perhaps pathological—intensity while embodying some of the central agonies of Lawrence's century. During Shaw's last years, in conversation with a neighbor, he made what may still be the most perceptive comment about *The Mint*'s meaning and significance. It showed, G.B.S. thought, the tragedy of sensitive men trapped in our time: "If like T. E. Lawrence, a sensitive man if ever there was one, they find themselves overwhelmed by the callousness and treachery of the machine, then they can lose their identity in the crowd and not think of themselves as separate egos."[16]

CHAPTER IV

"Chapman's Homer"

WHILE busy upon a translation of the *Odyssey*, T. E. Lawrence once noted wryly to a friend that his rendering might aptly be titled "Chapman's Homer." The friend understood. The allusion was not to the version immortalized in Keats's sonnet. As few knew, Lawrence's father, after leaving Ireland, had lived under another name than his real one of Chapman. Apprehensive about attempting an original new work after *The Mint* yet hoping to fasten upon a new writing project, Lawrence had begun thinking about a translation of Homer. In the solitude of Miranshah—a remote R.A.F. mountain base to which he had been transferred from Karachi—he began working on a version of the *Odyssey*. As Homer effectively occupied his small surplus of leisure, the first fifty lines came easily, but he worried over four drafts of the first book for a month. Bruce Rogers, an American book designer and illustrator, had agreed to commission a full translation if he liked a sample chapter, and Lawrence, eager to start another book, wanted the commission. As before, T.E. ran both from and toward a literary career.

Why work on the *Odyssey* appealed to Lawrence he may not even have known himself, but Jean Beraud Villars has suggested eloquently a possible subconscious reason:

We learn from the earliest sources that it is difficult to disband an army after a long campaign; the *Odyssey* is the story of the troubled demobilisation of a captain and his soldiers who after years of fighting are unable to return to a peaceful life, and whom war pursues beyond the war's end.

The soldier when freed, divests himself with difficulty of the character of a warrior, in which he has had a cruel but exciting time and above all a life with a simple and well-defined aim, a sort of moral comfort in servitude. Discipline is a hard pillow, but one on which heads in torment love to recline. What is more, the rediscovery of the fatherland, left so long before, seems to the demobilised soldier a sad disappointment. During the chaos of war the ideals for which he left to fight have not remained intact. He feels a foreigner in his own country, and finds that the community which he had defended is ruled by profiteers and greybeards. With bitterness he thinks: "Rome is no longer Rome."[1]

The *Odyssey* dragged into 1930, by which time T.E. was back at a base in England. Though he had finished Book xx and was four books from the end, Lawrence clearly had tired of the job. Bruce Rogers and Emery Walker were anxious to get the limited subscriber's edition underway so that the price could be fixed for solicitation of subscribers and booksellers, yet Rogers could not help but notice that Lawrence's enthusiasm for the project had grown weak. To Edward Garnett, Lawrence complained that the book took all his free time, including parts of his nights, and hoped it would be finished by the end of March, a year late. It would be a relief, he admitted: "I am tired of all Homer's namby-pamby men and women." An added indignity diminished his enthusiasm even more: Rogers had sent his translation (as far as it went) to an *Odyssey* expert who had suggested a series of corrections. Rogers insisted on them, and Lawrence gave in to most of them, while defending himself strenuously:

You may have thought me cavalier in preferring my own way. . . . Yet, actually, I'm in as strong a position vis-a-vis Homer as most of his translators. For years we were digging up a city of roughly the Odysseus period. I have handled the weapons, armour, utensils of those times, explored their houses, planned their cities. I have hunted wild boar and watched wild lions, sailed the Aegean (and sailed ships), bent bows, lived with pastoral peoples, woven textiles, built boats and killed many men. So I have odd knowledges that qualify me to understand the *Odyssey*, and odd experiences that interpret it to me. Therefore a certain headiness in rejecting help.[2]

Toward the close of 1932, Lawrence's *Odyssey*, with typography and decoration by Bruce Rogers and translation by "T. E. Shaw," was published. The translator had insisted that his "Lawrence" name was not to appear on the book, for he did not want people buying it on the strength of "Lawrence of Arabia's" reputation. Nevertheless, it is unlikely that many people who bought the book then did not know, through the publicity and the reviews, that the "T. E. Shaw" on the title page was Lawrence. Posthumous reprint editions bear both names.

Lawrence's "Translator's Note" which appeared as preface reflected his exasperation with Homer and with the drawn-out project, as well as his compulsive need to play the literary critic. The *Odyssey*, he explained, was no masterpiece like the *Iliad*, yet "by its ease and interest [it] remains the oldest book worth reading for its story and the first novel of Europe." Perhaps in self-exculpation he added, "The author misses his every chance of greatness, as must all his faithful translators." Homer, he thought, "lived too long after the heroic age to feel assured and large. He shows exact knowledge of what he could and could not do. Only through such superb self-criticism can talent rank beside inspiration."

In "four years of living with this novel" he had tried to deduce the author from his work and defiantly drew a Homer unlike that of popular tradition:

I found a bookworm, no longer young, living [far] from home, a mainlander, city-bred and domestic. Married but not exclusively, a dog-lover, often hungry and thirsty, dark-haired. Fond of poetry, a great if uncritical reader of the Iliad, with limited sensuous range but an exact eyesight which gave him all his pictures. A lover of old bric-a-brac, though as muddled an antiquary as Walter Scott—in sympathy with which side of him I have conceded "tenterhooks" but not railway-trains.

Lawrence found in Homer, too, what today would have to be labeled a male chauvinist in "his infuriating male condescension toward inglorious woman," who was less to him that any serving-man. And he found a love of the rural scene of a variety only common in the city-dweller, although his Homer ("no farmer") had "learned the points of a good olive tree." Lawrence's Homer was also more a stranger to the sword than the spade:

He is all adrift when it comes to fighting, and had not seen deaths in battle. He had sailed upon and watched the sea with a palpitant concern, seafaring being not his trade. As a minor sportsman he had seen wild boars at bay and heard tall yarns of lions.

Few men can be sailors, soldiers and naturalists. Yet this Homer was neither land-lubber nor stay-at-home nor ninny. He wrote for audiences to whom adventures were daily life and the sea their universal neighbour. So he dared not err. That famous doubled line where the Cyclops narrowly misses the ship with his stones only shows how much better a seaman he was than his copyist. Scholiasts have tried to riddle his technical knowledge

—and of course he does make a hotch-potch of periods. It is the penalty of being pre-archaeological.

Lawrence wondered (it was in part an explanation of his guarded method) whether some of the "queer naivety" he saw was irony. "At our remove of thought and language" he would not risk guessing how much intentional humor or satire Homer had supplied. He was baffled, he confessed, by a humble and seemingly unrefined dignity in the *Odyssey* because Homer could not have been "simple in education nor primitive socially." His evidence was internal:

His generation so rudely admired the Iliad that even to misquote it was a virtue. He sprinkles tags of epic across his pages. In this some find humour. Rather I judge that here too the tight lips of archaic art have grown the fixed grin of archaism.

Very bookish, this house-bred man. His work smells of the literary coterie, of a writing tradition. His notebooks were stocked with purple passages and he embedded these in his tale wherever they would more or less fit. . . . Fashion gave him recurring epithets, like labels: but repetitions tell, in public speaking. For recitation, too, are the swarming speeches. A trained voice can put drama and incident into speeches. Perhaps the tedious delay of the climax through ten books may be a poor bard's means of prolonging his host's hospitality.

Obviously the tale was the thing; and that explains (without excusing it to our ingrown minds) his thin and accidental characterisation. He thumbnailed well; and afterwards lost heart. Nausicaa, for instance, enters dramatically and shapes, for a few lines, like a woman—then she fades, unused. Eumaeus fared better: but only the central family stands out, consistently and pitilessly drawn—the sly cattish wife, that cold-blooded egotist Odysseus, and the priggish son who yet met his master-prig in Menelaus. It is sorrowful to believe that these were really Homer's heroes and examples.

T. E.'s paradoxes were at least free from the usual cant, and if we owe such provocative insights to his impatience with the project, the delays may have had their unlooked-for values.

Although many reviews of the translation appeared, T.E. was less interested in the reaction of others to it than he had been in the public response to his "personal" books, the *Seven Pillars* (and its abridgment) and *The Mint*. It was partly that the literary way of life was fading from him as he became absorbed in work on R.A.F. watercraft, and partly that he had (or circumstances had forced him to) let the work of translation drag on until he felt sated with Homer. Also, there had been unwanted literary advice—and distasteful pressure to accept it—from those who had commissioned the translation and then hesitated to trust the translator's scholarly authority in the matter. Still, he had collected six hundred pounds for the effort and was reasonably satisfied with his part of the book, though he was disappointed with Bruce Rogers' decorations. (Rogers' typography was beautiful, he wrote William Rothenstein, but he was "not fond of vase-painting.")

The *Odyssey* translation received favorable reviews both in the United States and in England. The *Sunday Times* (November 5, 1932) called it a "wonderful performance. . . . The greatest of all romantic tales has been rendered into English as rich and as rhythmically subtle as the original." The New York *Times* called it a "ruggedly and roughly masculine" translation, with a use of adjectives and adverbs that gave it "distinctive ornament and color." The *Book-of-the-Month Club News* recognized it as "one of the notable books of our time." More serious was the analysis—and the praise—of C. M. Bowra, one of the great classical scholars of Lawrence's age, who scrutinized it for the *New Statesman* with scholarly thoroughness:

Aircraftman Shaw was right to choose prose as his medium, because it is the natural medium for English narrative and the *Odyssey* is first and foremost a story. All verse translations of it have failed, because they are too literary and lose its essential freshness, and only in the prose of Malory has English any kind of parallel to this epic art. Indeed this translation is by far the best translation of Homer into English. It conveys more of his qualities and is infinitely more readable than Pope or Mackail or Butcher and Lang. It is not a crib, and the plodding student may at times be led astray by it but it stands on its own as literature and can be read for its own sake. It is as exciting, humorous, and technical as the *Odyssey* is. The muscular rhythm of its sentences is no poor substitute for the Homeric hexameter, and its complete lack of trite phrases and exhausted words gives it the youth and gaiety of Greek.

Aircraftman Shaw has lived with the *Odyssey* for years and come to know it with an intimacy denied to most scholars. He understands the world of which it tells and he moves easily among hunters and soldiers, weapons and ships. Therefore he brings a fresh mind to objects known to most men only from books. He takes Homer's stock description of a spear and translates "great, heavy, and close-grained, tipped with cutting bronze." That is absolutely literal and right, but no one has ever thought of it before. So, too, with a ship sailing: "The wind caught the sail, bellying it out, and the blue-shadowed waves resounded under the fore-feet of the running ship as she lay over on her course and raced out to sea." That is less literal, but no less right, and only a man used to ships would have written it. The result is that the *Odyssey* is freed from the dead burden of literature which hampers it in other translations. It can be read as the work of a living man.

Bowra was interested in how Lawrence solved two problems every translator of the *Odyssey* has had to face—how much in Homer is intentionally humorous, and how much archaism Homer himself used deliberately. Lawrence, he thought, had doubts even about intentional irony in Homer, for when Homer's Zeus called Aegisthus, the murderer of Agamemnon, "blameless," T.E. evaded the dilemma by substituting the word "great." There was far less evasion of the challenge to find modern equivalents to Homer's archaisms, and Bowra was pleased with the "skill and appropriateness" of the choices by which Lawrence retained a slight air of affectation without cost to the meaning. But the *Odyssey* was primarily a story, and he found Lawrence's rendering "admirable narrative," moving at the same pace as the original and deftly combining simplicity and affectation so that every word was "vital and engaging." Among the passages he quotes to make his point was one of the most picturesque in the story:

> As they talked a dog lying there lifted his head and pricked his ears. This was Argos whom Odysseus had bred but never worked, because he left for Ilium too soon. On a time the young fellows used to take him out to course the wild goats, the deer, the hares: but now he lay derelict and masterless on the dung-heap before the gates, on the deep bed of mule-droppings and cow-dung which collected there till the serfs of Odysseus had time to carry it off for manuring his broad acres. So lay Argos the hound, all shivering with dog-ticks.

The passage, Bowra concluded, "is familiar and famous, but the most assiduous scholar will find new light in the translation, so like it is to the original, so strong and lively in itself."[3]

It was high praise, but none of the praise in the press cheered Lawrence, who predictably (but privately) described his work as "manufactured writing," and consoled himself that its chief value was extraliterary. Publication of the *Odyssey* would assist in the culmination of his personal odyssey by providing him with funds for the refurbishing of Clouds Hill, his Dorset cottage, to prepare it for permanent occupancy when his enlistment would end.

Publicly, the translator presented a different face. Although he had begun his preface with the disclaimer that "The twenty-eighth English rendering of the Odyssey can hardly be called a literary event, especially when it aims to be essentially a straightforward translation," in the next line he confessed that when he was confronted with the choice "between a poor and a rich word," he opted for the opulent one, "to raise the colour." The *Odyssey* was to him "the oldest book worth reading for its story and the first novel of Europe." Novelist George Moore had said the same thing privately just a few years earlier, writing to his friend John Eglinton, "I am going to point out to you why all the translations of the *Odyssey* have failed. Because the translators have allowed the story to sink. The *Odyssey* is an objective poem and the story is everything, and the aim of the translator should be always to keep the story right up at the top of the orchestra." The important thing for Lawrence was to interest readers, not to choose among the scholarly subtleties of contested readings; yet he eschewed raciness and strove to preserve the merits of the original text, as he saw them, as closely as possible.

First to be confronted with Lawrence's philosophy of translation had been Ronald Storrs, who had come upon T.E. early in 1929 returning from India on the *Rajputana* and discovered that he had been spending his time in his bunk translating Homer. Storrs looked over what T.E. had written and told him that he "sacrificed overmuch to the desire of differing from predecessors." (Lawrence had, for example, rendered *rosy fingered dawn* nineteen different ways.) It was, Storrs thought, "an arresting rather than a satisfying version," and of Matthew Arnold's three requisites for translating Homer—simplicity, speed, and nobility—he thought Lawrence had failed in the third.[4] T.E. listened and made no objection. Nor did he make any changes.

Weighing English translations a generation after Lawrence, Kimon Friar—himself guilty of one—divided them into

prose literal (Buckley, Cary, Morgan, Murray), prose "rhythmical" (Palmer), prose pseudo-archaic (Butcher and Lang)... prose colloquial (Butler, Rouse, Rieu) ... [couplets] of rhymed pentameter (Chapman, Ogilsby, Sotheby), of rhymed heptameter (di Cane), and of heroic breed (Fenton, Pope, Giles); into blank verse plain (Hobbes, Norgate) ... and into blank verse Miltonic (Cowper, Wright); into iambic-anapestic pentameter (Andrew, Lindsey), and hexameter (Way, Morris, Grylls); and into ballad measure (Newman, Maginn), quatrain rhymed (Gladstone), quatrain Rubaiyat (Mackail), and, of course, into the "original meter" (Cotterill, Caulfield, Schumann).[5]

Friar called Lawrence's redaction "prose wrought"—the "wrought prose of a man of action brooding on style: often artificed, but often swift and splendid."[6] Elsewhere Lawrence's version is seen as in the line of the post-Victorian reaction against archaism, which at its extreme "purged Homer so effectively of his formulaic quirks and formulaic repetitions that most of the poetry vanished at the same time."[7] This practice established the primacy of story over poetry, of narrative over language—the practice of Butler and Rieu, between whom Lawrence, with his attempts to merge colloquialism and artifice in a prose version, appears to provide a link. Its major virtue seems to have been noted early by David Garnett in pointing out to Lawrence (in a thank-you note for a copy of the book) that it was "full of the beauty of solid things."[8] Lawrence worked with his hands and could transform the verses in which Odysseus builds a vessel with which to leave Calypso's shores into a piece of elevated technical writing:

First she gave him a great axe of cutting copper, well-suited to his reach. It was ground on both edges and into the socketed head firmly edged the well-rounded handle of olive-wood. Then she gave him a finished smoothing-adze and led the way to the end of the island where the trees grew tall, the alders and the poplars with heaven-scaling pines, withered long since and sapless and very dry, which would float high for him. She showed him where the loftiest trees had grown, did Calypso that fair goddess: then she returned to her cavern while he busily cut out his beams, working with despatch. Twenty trees in all he threw and axed into shape with the sharp copper, trimming them adeptly and trueing them against his straight-edge. Then his lovely goddess brought to him augers with which he bored the logs for lashing together: firmly he fastened them with pegs and ties. As broad as a skilled shipwright would design and lay down the floor of a roomy merchant ship, just so full in beam did Odysseus make his raft. To carry his upper deck he set up many ribs, closely kneed and fitted, and he united the heads of these with long rubbing-strakes, for gunwales. He put a mast into his craft, with a yard in proportion: also a stern sweep with which to steer her. To defend himself from breaching seas he fenced in the sides of the raft with wicker work, wattling it cunningly all of osiers like a basket and adding a lavish reinforcement of stanchions. Calypso came again with a bolt of cloth for sails, which he stitched strongly. Then he set up stays and sheets and halyards, and at last with levers he worked the raft down into the sacred sea. By the fourth evening the work ended.[9]

Although Lawrence, a self-exile even in his own land (and a true exile, in the mountains of Kashmir during much of the writing), had a special sympathy with the travail of Odysseus, his changing R.A.F. environments and the nature of the book's commission did not augur for a particularly inspired translation. Perhaps his version's triumph lies in its being as effective as it is, apart from the interest inherent in one compulsive adventurer's rendering of another's adventure. Few translations are for all time, and his "Be mum now and see that never a one of you speaks to me" contains at least one word not a candidate for permanency. Still, Lawrence's version flags less often than most translations, however much he ignored the Homeric oral style: and his translation not only continues to go through renewed reprintings (partly, perhaps, because beneath "T. E. Shaw" on the title page the publishers have added "Lawrence of Arabia") but is utilized in its own right by scholars. In 1970, a photographic and textual re-creation of the voyage of Ulysses, for which Erich Lessing traveled four thousand miles along a route developed from Homer's descriptions, was published.[10] For his English text the author used that of T. E. Shaw.

In Lawrence's own time one admirer of his *Odyssey* suggested that he go on to translate the *Iliad*. In his first week as a civilian (and in the last months of his life) he answered self-deprecatingly in the negative. "The Iliad is a poem and as untranslatable as Paradise Lost. No great poem has ever been translated—yet. The poor little Odyssey is a mere novel, and need not lose . . . in the process. All the same my version has no intrinsic merits."[11] Referring to the "wound and the bow" image made famous by Edmund Wilson, a classical scholar has written, "If the core of darkness in Lawrence cannot be understood without the metaphor of Philoctetes, his splendor as a human being and a writer cannot be understood without the metaphors of the *Odyssey* and the *Iliad*. Both of these poems enter into his experiences, his writings, and into shaping his outlook. Homer was a lifelong study with Lawrence and he emerges as one of his finest translators."[12] Nothing short of a subject with epical potential appealed to Lawrence, and if the subject did not emerge of itself, Lawrence seized an epic in hand. Thus the *Odyssey*. But after that, what? His ambitions as a writer required something worth his feeding upon. In an unheroic age his dilemma forced him back upon himself, and even there no resolution was in sight, for he was deliberately living the unheroic life.

CHAPTER V

The Would-be Literary Critic

IN 1921, when T.E. was a fellow of All Souls'
and Robert Graves an undergraduate at St. John's, the young
poet visited his new friend's rooms almost daily, often to use
T.E. as a literary sounding board. "He reminded me,"
Graves recalled in his concluding lecture as professor of
poetry at Oxford in 1965, "that resounding invectives by
young men against sacrosanct literary idols are always con-
strued as jealousy or spite. The only effective way to rock
their pedestals, he said, was by quoting pejorative textual and
domestic details—the smaller and more particular the better
—which would suggest that, though idols, they were not the
sort of men whom one would invite to breakfast in one's
rooms or trust with one's cat while away on holiday."[1] The
suggestion smacked more of critical bad manners than critical
integrity; but it is only one of many indications that Lawrence could have been one of his era's shrewdest critics. There
are other evidences that he wishfully harbored such ambitions.

"The idea of my posing as an arbiter of letters," Lawrence wrote a friend in 1931, "is absurd, and preposterous and uncouth and ungodly and un-everything else. A retired Colonel who wrote his memoirs."[2] Nevertheless his letters, as early as those of his college years, are full of critical observations about writers and writing, and his postwar correspondence, a major portion of which was to creative writers and critics, is about other writers and critics. It would be possible to compile a substantial book of criticism from these comments in the published and unpublished letters, some of them detailed critical essays.* A number of the letters are critical analyses sent directly, in friendship, to the authors themselves, some less than honest in their flattery, others perhaps too honest for the author's comfort. About an unpublished story sent to him by E. M. Forster, for example, he wrote, "I don't expect you to be always at your best. Indeed I once said that it was the mark of a little writer to be very particular about his standard. The big men (of the Balzac, Tolstoi, Dostoevski stamp) are incredibly careless. . . . There's a lavish ease about their stuff: and an agony of carefulness about the Henry James & George Moore & Flaubert class."[3]

Lawrence might have liked to think that he belonged in the former class; in any event he was lavish—and often careless—in his epistolary criticism. "He was wayward," critic F. L. Lucas—a friend— has written, "and hence could make wild remarks. . . . On the other hand, being so brilliant, he could sometimes make very penetrating judgments. . . . And I think he was prone to grow over-enthusiastic about young

* A few of the more lengthy comments are extracted in the slim *Men in Print*, together with a sampling of T.E.'s *Spectator* reviews edited by A. W. Lawrence and published in a limited edition by the Golden Cockerel Press in 1940.

writers who personally caught his fancy."[4] When this happened, the T.E.L. reputation could be a rocket-launcher. Poet
Laureate (in the late sixties and seventies) Cecil Day Lewis,
for example, had been little known as a poet until "Aircraftman Shaw" was reported by a gossip columnist in 1934 as
having mentioned to Winston Churchill that Day Lewis was
a good prospect. "Hardly had the newspaper come out," the
poet recalled in amazement, "when the telephone bell started
ringing in the office of the Hogarth Press. Leonard and Virginia Woolf [the proprietors], having sold the usual small
number of each of my three books of verse they had so far
published, had covered the stack of unsold copies with chintz
—or so the story goes—and were using it as a settee. The
orders now pouring in for these books caused Leonard and
Virginia to subside until, within a few hours, they were sitting on the floor."[5] Day Lewis' next volume sold well from
the start, but two friends wrote to him in warning. Edwin
Muir told him to be wary of becoming facile and careless,
and Lawrence warned him that "poets hope too much," and
to leave politics to the politicians. Ruefully, Day Lewis confessed later that the advice "had only a delayed action upon
me, for the results of leaving politics to the politicians of the
Thirties were all too disastrously in evidence all around us."[6]

Another poet who benefited from Lawrence's praise (a
decade earlier) was Roy Campbell. Augustus John had shown
T.E. the manuscript of Campbell's *The Flaming Terrapin*, and
T.E. was impressed. "I think this is a coming thing," he
wrote to publisher Jonathan Cape, enclosing the manuscript.
The poet, he noted, was "a believer in Keats and Shelley and
Moby Dick, with other influences visible:—but the thing is
very good."[7] It was the start of Campbell's stormy career.

Another time Lawrence "tried hard" to get E. E. Cummings' *Enormous Room* published in England, but "Cape wouldn't touch it; nor could [agent] Curtis Brown, who touted it round with a very cautious little note from me, place it anywhere. I call it one of the very best of the war books."[8]

Others benefited from Lawrence's private criticism and literary intervention, but his published critical output remained small. The first critical piece he published under his own name was an introduction to the Medici Society 1921 reprint of Charles Doughty's *Travels in Arabia Deserta*, a travel classic T.E. revered. Doughty, old and in frail fiscal health, needed the income, and only a "Lawrence of Arabia" introduction made the reprint possible. With kindness Lawrence wrote to Doughty, "I feel this is as absurd as it would be to introduce Shakespeare. However they urged that I had an advertisement value . . . and so I said that I would do it, if you would allow it to be done. I'm afraid you will feel it rather an outrage on the book."[9]

What he wrote was a personal piece, beginning, "It is not comfortable to have to write about 'Arabia Deserta.' I have studied it for ten years, and have grown to consider it a book not like other books, but something particular, a bible of its kind." Although the rest was praise, privately Lawrence had second thoughts about Doughty's style, especially after discovering critical reaction to the obvious influence of *Arabia Deserta* on his own *Seven Pillars*. The style of *Arabia Deserta* was in one way self-defeating, he wrote David Garnett in 1927: "I regret Doughty's style, and find it unjustifiable; not that his skill in using it does not justify him, as a verbal artist, in using it, but because the difficulty of it had barred so many readers from what is, after all, much more than a piece of verbal art. Philologically, too, he is all wrong; why should we borrow our syntax from the Sweden or Denmark of 80 years ago?"[10]

Later, T.E. provided a preface to Richard Garnett's *The Twilight of the Gods* (1924) and a foreword to Bertram Thomas' *Arabia Felix: Across the Empty Quarter of Arabia* (1932). There would have been many more, as his name in a preface could have turned almost anyone's manuscript into selling copy; but he resisted all other blandishments. When Sir Ronald Storrs asked him to write a preface to a book by a Storrs acquaintance, he bristled, "No: I won't; forewords are septic things, and I hope never to do another. Bertram Thomas was like the importunate woman, but to strangers it is easy to say 'No.'"[11] As part of his intermittent literary hack-work he wrote flap-copy puffs for Cape books and even edited, anonymously, another traveler's journal of experiences in Syria, asking for payment in the form of books Cape would have sent him for the asking anyway.

Since he needed the money, T.E. eventually agreed to do some criticism for publication. Francis Yeats-Brown, assistant editor of the *Spectator* in the mid-twenties, had asked him to review books on the Middle East. Characteristically, T.E. agreed to review books occasionally—but on any subject but Arabia, and only under a pseudonym. "Reviewing comes hard to me," he wrote, and added—strangely, considering his passion for criticism-laden correspondence—"I can't do it without trying my best: and if I've ever in my past written decently it was under dire command of some mastering need to put on paper a case, or a relation, or an explanation, of something I cared about. I don't see that happening with literature."

Insisting upon anonymity, Lawrence suggested the identifying initials "C.D."—for "Colin Dale," he explained, thus distancing himself even from the pseudonym which might have seemed sufficient to satisfy a passion for privacy. Colin Dale to the uninitiated may have sounded like a name out of *Robin Hood*, or perhaps drawn from an early English pastoral. But Colindale—the pseudonym run together—was to Lawrence the station on the London underground (actually above ground at that point) closest to Hendon Aerodrome. And T.E. was "Aircraftman Shaw."

With complete seriousness, T.E. then explained to Yeats-Brown how his full pseudonym should be revealed to the public—as if it were the revelation of an authentic identity. "I suggest," he wrote, "the first five or six things worth publishing be restrained to their initials. If the miracle continues after that (surely either your forbearance or my endeavor will break down) we might climb so far as Colin D., keeping the full truth about the D till it was certain that the fellow could write and had a character. In my heart of hearts I know he hasn't."[12]

He may have wanted to try out a new pseudonym or perhaps establish a separate reputation as a critic so that he could assure himself that his writing was not being accepted only because it was signed by Lawrence of Arabia. If so, his first review as "C.D."—of a collected editon of D. H. Lawrence's novels[13]—was a successful experiment. Immediately on publication an editor wrote to the *Spectator* asking about the identity of the reviewer, and suggesting that "C.D." edit a volume for them. Those who knew T.E. might have guessed his hand, for he had a passion for typography and for the appearance of the printed page:

Martin Secker has been too careful in producing his cheap edition of D. H. Lawrence's novels. In its clumsy type-panel the type looks too big, and the reverse looms shadowly through the thin paper: also the margins have been pared to the quick. This is a pity, for D. H. Lawrence is a prodigious novelist, whose works need to be studied in series (to learn their significance of growth) as well as to be re-read frequently, each for itself, because of the rich depth and strangeness and fine artistry of the author. These little volumes are likely to crack up under the work book-lovers will give them.[14]

The appearance of a collected editon is usually the occasion for a retrospective view, and T.E. used it to imply some things about himself while he analyzed, with great perception, D. H. Lawrence and E. M. Forster:

In those early days, before the War, readers' hopes lay in Lawrence and Forster. These two heirs, through the Victorians, of the great tradition of the English novel were fortunate to have made good their footing before war came. Its bursting jarred their stride, indeed. Lawrence glances at the War twice or thrice, and wrote a haunting poem of a train-journey in uniform, but no more. Each man had tired of politics and action, and plunged into the dim forest of character in time to save himself from chaos. In imagination we used to make Forster and Lawrence joust with one another, on behalf of their different practices of novel-writing, as our fathers set Thackeray and Dickens at odds. Forster's world seemed a comedy, neatly layered and staged in a garden whose trim privet hedges were delicate with gossamer conventions. About its lawns he rolled thunderstorms in teacups, most lightly, beautifully. Lawrence painted hussies and bounders, unconscious of class, with the unabashed surety of genius, whether they were in their slippered kitchens or others' drawingrooms. Forster's characters were typical. Lawrence's were individual. "There have been enough stories about ordinary people." said he in self-defence: but it was easy for him to say that. Everybody in the world would be remarkable, if we used all our eyes to see them. Lawrence will call one eloquent, because his body curves interestingly when he stands still. Another is rich, because his dark silence means something. A third may thrill, once in the book, in voice. Some have interesting minds. Not many.

Forster may love a character, in a gentle, aloof irony of love, like a collector uncovering his pieces of price for a moment to a doubtful audience, as if he feared that an untaught eye might soil, by not comprehending, their fineness. Lawrence is a showman, trumpeting his stock, eager for us to make them ours—at his price. There is no comedy in him. He prods their ribs, pries open their jaws to show the false teeth. It is not very comfortable, on first reading. To be impassive spectators of the slave-market takes a training.

Forster is clever and subtle. Lawrence is not subtle, though he tries, sometimes, to convey emotional subtlety. In the big things his simplicity is shattering. His women browbeat us, as Juno browbeat the Gods at Jupiter's at-homes: but in the privacy of their dressingrooms they jabber helplessly. Pages and pages are wasted in the efforts to make the solar plexus talk English prose.[15]

After the D. H. Lawrence review there were others through the latter part of 1927 and into 1928, the best of them one titled "Hakluyt—First Naval Propagandist,"[16] and another on H. G. Wells's collected short stories.[17] The Wells critique was as interesting for what it intimated about T. E. Lawrence, but it was nevertheless a substantial assessment of Wells as a writer of short fiction. As an author who felt "dry as a squeezed orange," T.E. was fascinated by Wells's ability to turn out so much writing of all kinds that the sixty-three stories in the volume only represented it fractionally. "His drafts," T.E. mused, "would tell us if this huge production is due to industry or to a happy fluency. His writings let us into so many workshops and laboratories that we would like to see his own."

The tales provided the opportunity, T.E. continued, "to distinguish the profile of H. G. Wells, the prose artist," for in the mature novelist "we cannot see the writer for the dust of his manly activities." Wells, he thought, spared little admiration "for pure writing, which he thinks a fad of emasculate amateurs. Yet he cannot keep out of his work that secret rhythm which its sentences (bare of relative clauses, and dependents, and adjectives, and participles) hold somewhere in their structure. So that any person with an ear and knowledge of letters, after about six lines, says 'Wells,' and is right every time."

T.E. mourned the failure of the publisher to date each tale, or to print them chronologically, so that one could consider Wells, "as a growth, like an oak-tree." And he discovered a scientific humility in Wells, who in his short fiction was "prepared to hold everything as possible—the genuine, unmixed humility of the student-investigator on the threshhold of science. There is not a trace of the professorial mood, and no presumption of deep knowledge." But there were traces of Wells's literary antecedents, and T.E. sensed them acutely, from Poe to Wilde and Kipling; and he saw in one magical tale, "The Door in the Wall," a precursor of Forster, almost (if such were possible in advance) "a gloss on an E. M. Forster fragment." Above all, he saw the Wells of the short fiction as a "craftsman," a term T.E. used only in the highest sense. "For exact subordination of means few English writers better earn the attribute classical—in his short stories. In the novels, his men and women sometimes mutiny and exceed his plan."

Yeats-Brown sent a cutting of the columns to Wells, and Wells—whether cautiously or honestly—described "C.D.'s" review as "the most interesting estimate of his work that he had ever seen."[18] But T.E. complained to Robert Graves, possibly dishonestly, that he had spent three days of his Christmas holiday on the Wells review, "and they have been wasted . . .: I can't write reviews, yet want to, badly!"[19] Certainly the latter element of the complaint was sincere, whatever else he might have wanted to do with his Christmas at a time when he almost never left his base for any reason whatever.

"Colin Dale's" enthusiasm for regular reviewing clearly was waning; yet it was remarkable that he was able to do any of it at all, considering his situation as an R.A.F. ranker in India half a world away from the London literary scene he loved yet ran from. T.E. produced little other criticism after that; one effort, a piece intended for the *Spectator* early in 1928 but printed only posthumously, was an essay-review of a collected edition of Walter Savage Landor. Again the passion for good printing was sufficiently dominant to appear early in the essay. Lawrence wrote, "Here is all Landor or all enough. It is magnificently printed, in a type of excellence, on good paper, in a size which is imposing, as Landor should be, without being unwieldy. I have carried its various volumes about with me, lately trying to think out a review of them, and have not suffered either from their weight or size. The binding is apparently strong. A car wheel passed over Volume three, without its disintegrating."[20]

But Lawrence was also unafraid of making critical judgments:

A great artist: he said his say beautifully. The cadences of his prose, the lambent smiling of the old thing, the ripeness of age, the prejudices and cocksureness of too long a life, are all here, perfectly set down. His art was such another vehicle as the prose of George Moore: a vehicle which was so lovely itself that (for a long time) no one asks where it is going, or whether it is going anywhere. For a long time:—but for sixteen volumes? Not for me.

It's as lovely, and as remote, and as useless, as the sound that wind makes in the top of too close a grove of firs. A music of whispering, which steals down the cathedral-dark, pillared, yet starved trunks within the grove. It is good to listen there, once in a way. We may be sure that whenever we walk there, the music of the wind will be waiting there for us, as in a store:

but it's a pleasure which, if made an end, wouldn't help us very much. It is too smooth, too sure, too unfaltering to hold much mind.[21]

Why T.E. gave up literary criticism of a public variety* is uncertain. It would have further complicated his life had he continued to write criticism from the distance of India—and even more complicated it had he used his own name. Unquestionably he preferred, too, the secret joys of private criticism communicated to friends influential in the literary establishment and the secret power of making, or helping to make, a new reputation through his quiet intervention. Had he had a more extended post-R.A.F. life, however, there might have been a good deal more seen of the half-concealed, would-be critic.

* His translator's note to the *Odyssey*, written in 1931, is an interesting exception. Published under the name T. E. Shaw, it nevertheless enjoyed only token pseudonymity; nor did the publisher attempt to conceal its authorship.

CHAPTER VI

Translator and Poet

L AWRENCE'S ambivalent attitude toward money included refusing just about all writing income he could have earned as "Lawrence of Arabia" but now and then, when hard-pressed, accepting writing assignments of a hack variety, if the results could be published anonymously or under pseudonyms (thus his *Spectator* reviews). Yet if he were not "Lawrence of Arabia" such pseudonymous assignments would not have been forthcoming. In this way he solicited from his *Revolt in the Desert* publisher Jonathan Cape[1] several assignments to do translations from the French. One Cape offered was Mardrus' version of *The Arabian Nights*. T.E. was eager (within his usual limits): "I've lots of time, and could do up to two thousand very decent words a day. Anonymous, of course." But when Cape went to the French publisher for rights to translate he found that they had been recently granted elsewhere. Next he offered Lawrence *Le Gigantesque*, Adrien le Corbeau's unusual "biography" of a giant tree, and Lawrence started work on it in the summer of 1923. "This is how *Le Gigantesque* stands," he wrote Cape in July. "I started gaily, did about twenty pages into direct swinging English, then turned back and read it, and it was horrible. The bones of the poor thing showed through. I did it again more floridly. The book is written very common-placedly by a man of good imagination, and a bad mind, an unobservant. Consequently it is banal in style and ordinary in thought, and very interesting in topic."

By September 13 the translation was done; it was published in 1924 by Cape as *The Forest Giant*, translated by "J. H. Ross," T.E.'s first service pseudonym. To Bernard Shaw, on presenting him with a copy, T.E. wrote: "Straw isn't really necessary in brickmaking: and likewise it may not be the duty of a translator to better his text: but whenever I read any such book as this I can't help wishing that the idea had occurred to me first. It's probably as well it didn't."[2] To Edward Garnett earlier he had been more blunt about his work along those lines: "I disbelieve in my own products. And better do nothing than make Giantesques."[3] To Cape, however, he confided that his version was better than le Corbeau's—"but dishonest here and there" because "my stomach turned. Couldn't help it."

Despite such outward misgivings, Lawrence had been happy with the translation work, which took him out of his brooding about being mired at Bovington Camp, in the tank corps, when he yearned for the satisfactions of the R.A.F. Translation—as he had indicated to Jonathan Cape—had turned him, too, away from the self-consciously literary style of *Seven Pillars*. "Do you know," he wrote to Edward Garnett on October 4, 1923, "that lately I have been finding my deepest satisfaction in the collocation of words so ordinary and plain that they cannot mean anything to a book-jaded mind: and out of some of such I can draw deep stuff. Is it perhaps that certain sequences of vowels or consonants imply more than others: that writing of this sort has music in it? I don't want to affirm it, and yet I would not deny it: for if writing can have sense . . . and sound why shouldn't it have something of pattern too?" What he had been discovering in translation—especially when thrown upon his own resources in a barracks existence—is that he could eschew second-hand effects. "My sequences," he explained, "seem to be independent of ear . . . to impose themselves through the eye alone. I achieved a good many of them in *Le Gigantesque*: but fortuitously for the most part."

Curiously, the first words of *The Forest Giant* are "The Odyssey"—the title of the first chapter. Some years later, as "T. E. Shaw" rather than "J. H. Ross," he began a translation of the *Odyssey*. In the case of le Corbeau's book, the odyssey was not of a man but of a seed:*

For years on end it had been rolling, across the plains, through the deep meadow grasses, under the dim echoing archways of the forest. Always, in heat and cold, beneath blue skies, or skies clouded with rain and hail and snow, it had been rolling ceaselessly. One day it would be gilded by the sunlight—but not softened; another day grizzled streaks of rain soaked it— without refreshment. It was buried, to all appearances for ever, by drifts of snow—but was not hurt. It had crossed cataracts of light and floods of shadow; it had been rocked by soft winds and hurled dizzily into the air by the shrieking gusts of cyclones; and it had met all these things—the sweetness of the day, the shade of night, the winters, the springs, the summers— with the same submissive, invulnerable apathy. It had waited its hours, ready, if need be, to wait yet much longer.

* Of California *Sequoia*.

The opening paragraph is a reasonable sample of the mannered prose of the whole. The effort to sustain it undoubtedly wearied Lawrence; yet the book's tone, in spite of his dismissal of it as "ordinary in thought," must have found a sympathetic chord in Lawrence. One passage summed up a side of him never expressed better in any of his other writings:

Elements seem to grow tired at last of being confined in one special shape, to be weary of being so long a man, a stone, a river, a fire. Their weariness is ours, in sum. We feel vigorous or weak, joyful or sad, perturbed or resigned according to the prosperity of our cells: and we all, whatever our age and health, encounter hours in which, without reason given, our whole being longs for annihilation. At other times—in common experience it happens often at that hour when lamps should be lit—there swells up in us an indeterminate wish to be other than we are: and our flesh goes dead, our hearts cold, our heads empty of desire.

T.E.'s next venture in translation was self-aborted. Cape had offered him, when *The Forest Giant* was in press, another French book of an unusual type, *Sturly* by Pierre Custot, a depiction of ocean life viewed from an undersea perspective. "It will take a while to do well," Lawrence explained to Cape, "for the wretched man catalogues innumerable French fishes and my French never extended into scientific icthyology! Can you give me a long time to do it in? I'm hiring a writing room, giving up the struggle to do it in barracks." On Christmas Day, 1923, he wrote Cape that he had wanted to send the completed work as a Christmas present, but that it was not yet ready. "I'm afraid I'm no good as a translator," he confided, "indeed what the hell I am good for God only knows." A month later he wrote again: "To-night I have read through my *Sturly*, and have burned it page by page. There is something about this book which I cannot get. I have spent days over a single chapter and yet not got the essence of any [chapter]. I enclose a cheque for £20, add this to what you would have paid me and have a first-rate version done by a real, proper writer. It was not fair to the author and I like the book for that hard, unsentimental writing."

Cape returned T.E.'s check, offering him instead a commission to translate *Salammbo* for a new edition of Flaubert, but on February 21, 1924, T.E.—without returning the money this time—replied with a guarded *no*: "*Salammbo* . . . yes, I'd like to, there also . . . but what if I fail there? Failures, however they gratify my private judgement, are matters of pounds to you. I don't think the gamble justifiable. If your Flaubert was ready without *Salammbo*, what a lop-sided set it would be."

It was Lawrence's later debunker Richard Aldington who was ironically commissioned to do the aborted translation of *Sturly*. When the book appeared, its jacket copy was written by Lawrence. Other than the *Odyssey*, the only translation of Lawrence's published afterwards was a thin volume titled *Two Arabic Folk Tales*—and it appeared posthumously in 1937. It was hardly of recent vintage: T.E. had written the translations into a diary he had kept in northern Arabia in 1911.

Although the deliberate prose-poetry of many of the lines in *Seven Pillars* is palpable ("Day was still young as we rode between two great pikes of sandstone to the foot of a long, soft slope poured down from the domed hills"), there is almost no verse among his lesser writings, and his major attempt in the genre remains the strange dedicatory poem to *Seven Pillars*. It is cryptically entitled "To S.A."; hardly a word in its twenty-one lines has failed to cause speculation since its publication, and no certain identity of the dedicatee has been proved. Lawrence himself in a manuscript note once confessed, "dedication of book is to an imaginary person of neutral sex." Still, it is probable that "S.A." was actually Salim Achmed, a young Arab whom Lawrence had met in Carchemish and who died (apparently of typhoid) in Damascus during the war. In what seems a clear reference to him, Lawrence wrote a penciled note on a blank page at the end of Robert Vansittart's *The Singing Caravan*: "I wrought for him freedom to lighten his sad eyes: but he had died waiting for me. So I threw my gift away and now not anywhere will I find rest and peace. Written [in May, 1919] between Paris and Lyons in [a] Handley Page [aircraft]."[4]

Erroneously called "Sheik" Achmed in most writings about Lawrence, and often known as "Dahoum," Salim Achmed had been treated as a younger brother by Lawrence, who even brought him to stay with his parents in Oxford in 1913; and he accompanied Lawrence and Newcombe on their Sinai expedition. There is no evidence of carnality in his relationship with Lawrence, whatever the ambiguous suggestions of the published version of the "S.A." poem, which in its original form seems to describe Lawrence's coming upon his young friend as he lay dying and holding him briefly in his arms. (That such an incident occurred on one of Lawrence's trips behind the lines is attested to by gunner Tom Beaumont, who was then serving with Lawrence.[5]) Lawrence's first lines for the poem were drafted in 1919 and seem to establish their inspiration as the death of Achmed in Syria during the war: "I wrought for him freedom to lighten his sad eyes."[6]

Unsure of his versifying powers, Lawrence had asked Robert Graves to doctor his completed draft, and Graves

made some radical changes in diction and word order; he
retained Lawrence's sentimental use of Ahmed as a symbol
of captive yet emerging Arab nationhood while subtly (and
perhaps inadvertently) shifting the poem's tone. This is best
seen when the poems are read together:

[Lawrence's original draft[7]]

I loved you, so I drew these tides of men into my hands
    and wrote my will across the sky in stars
To gain you Freedom, the seven-pillared worthy house,
    that your eyes might be shining for me
                When we came.
Death was my servant on the road, till we were near
                and saw you waiting:
When you smiled, and in sorrowful envy he outran me
                and took you apart:
                    Into his quietness.
So our love's earnings was your cast-off body to be held
                one moment
Before earth's soft hands would explore your face and the
                blind worms transmute
                Your failing substance.
Men prayed me to set my work, the inviolate house,
                in memory of you.
But for fit monument I shattered it, unfinished: and now
The little things creep out to patch themselves hovels
                in the marred shadow
                  Of your gift.

[Graves's revision as published]

I loved you, so I drew these tides of men into my hands
    and wrote my will across the sky in stars
To earn you Freedom, the seven-pillared worthy house,
    that your eyes might be shining for me
                When we came.
Death seemed my servant on the road, till we were near
                and saw you waiting:
When you smiled, and in sorrowful envy he outran me

> and took you apart:
> Into his quietness.
> Love, the way-weary, groped for your body, our brief wage
> ours for the moment
> Before earth's soft hand explored your shape, and the blind
> worms grew fat upon
> Your substance.
> Men prayed me that I set our work, the inviolate house,
> as a memory of you.
> But for fit monument I shattered it, unfinished: and now
> The little things creep out to patch themselves hovels
> in the marred shadow
> Of your gift.

Essentially the poem as published remains Lawrence's, and the controversy over whether it is a symbolic reference to the Arab "nation" or a personal testament obscures what may be the considerable power the lines have as a poem autonomous of its use and location in *Seven Pillars*. Did Graves improve the poem? It is the same question as whether Shaw's editing of *Seven Pillars* enhanced the Oxford version. Lawrence's acceptance of the changes made them effectively his own.

Less pretentious in its grace and simplicity is the four-line adaptation of an Arabic poem by King Feisal which Lawrence did for Edward Marsh ("if you keep unstained the honour of your house"),[8] prefixed to this volume as epigraph; and there is a seventeen-line poem in free verse, "Confession of Faith," dated by David Garnett as 1929 and first published in 1951.[9] Possibly it was intended as a continuation of *The Mint*, for it evokes air force service in *Mint*-like concrete images, celebrating "soiled overalls" (the "livery" of the R.A.F.) as it celebrates speed and the effects of flight: "Our bodies cannot scale the heavens except in a fume of petrol.

The concentration of our bodies in entering a loop. Bones, blood, flesh all pressed inward together. . . . In speed we hurl ourselves beyond the body."[10]

A few years earlier Lawrence had chanced sending some of his poetry to Charlotte Shaw for criticism. He knew that G.B.S. had little interest in poetry, and he was too timid about his poetic talents to regularly entrust his verses to practiced hands among his friends. Her answer gives some clue to the nature of his experiments in poetry, and her tact suggests more than it says:

How about this:—
> The years like great big oxen tread the world
> And God the herdsman goads them on behind.

(I blush to say this line makes me giggle.)

The nearest I can get to your splendid line. It is Yeats. I do not yet know which of his poems it comes from,* but shall presently find it. I think it must have been this, lingering in your mind, [which] caused you to compose "My thoughts like slow black oxen crowd the plain," which is incomparably better than Yeats; my only criticism of it being that I never saw oxen crowd a plain. They always seem to come single spies (or dual), not in battalions.[11]

Clearly, T.E. was more a poet in his earlier prose, and his newer attempts reflected memory more than imagination; but his few extended experiments in verse demonstrate that he was in tune with the advanced writing of his time. What he could have done might be projected from his performance; what he *would* have done, given encouragement and years, we cannot know. The desire was there.

---

* Charlotte Shaw, quoting from memory from Yeats's *The Countess Cathleen*, was slightly inaccurate ("The years like great *black* oxen . . . ").

CHAPTER VII

Last Writings

IN his last years Lawrence restlessly cast about seeking writing subjects, but the internal pressure to write was never sufficiently concentrated or intense. Colonel Ralph Isham tried but failed to interest him in editing the vast Malahide Castle Boswell papers and in writing a biography of Mohammed. Jonathan Cape suggested that he undertake a biography of Doughty, and John Buchan wanted him to do one of Alexander the Great. Several friends sought to interest him in writing a biography of Roger Casement, and he may have intended to do so after his retirement from the air force. Before his retirement, in 1933, he tried—in vain—to convince Air Marshal Geoffrey Salmond to permit him to "do a long flying-boat voyage and write a log of it," a contribution to what he hoped would be a "Hakluyt for the air."[1]

Lawrence actually began what seems to have been planned as a sequel to, or continuation of, *The Mint*. A few penciled pages survive, apparently written between 1926 and 1931, each immediately after the event described. Several of them appear in print as vignettes sandwiched among the correspondence in David Garnett's edition of the *Letters*. On the manuscript Lawrence had inserted a title: "Leaves in the Wind."[2] The first was apparently written on board ship en route to R.A.F. service in India in December, 1926. On the evidence of the fragments Lawrence was still writing in the mood of *The Mint*. In one passage he is on sentry duty in Married Quarters on the troopship *Derbyshire*, in the corridor leading to the women's latrine. A stench pervades the corridor, and Lawrence hears the sound of splashing in the direction of the odor. Peering into the latrine he discovers that the drain is clogged and the floor flooded. The Orderly Officer comes by, and Lawrence reports the problem:

> The grimy-folded face, the hard jaw, toil-hardened hands. An ex-naval warrant, I'll bet. No gentleman. He strides boldly to the latrine: "Excuse me" unshyly to two shrinking women. "God," he jerked out, "flooded with shit—where's the trap?" He pulled off his tunic and threw it at me to hold, and with a plumber's quick glance strode over to the far side, bent down, and ripped out a grating. Gazed a moment, while the ordure rippled over his boots. Up his right sleeve, baring a fore arm hairy as a mastiff's grey leg, knotted with veins, and a gnarled hand; thrust it deep in, groped, pulled out a moist white bundle. "Open that port" and out it splashed into the night. "You'd think they'd have had some other place for their sanitary towels. Bloody awful show, not having anything fixed up." He shook his sleeve down as it was over his slowly-drying arm, and huddled on his tunic, while the released liquid gurgled contentedly down its re-opened drain.[3]

The drive behind such passages, R. P. Blackmur has suggested, "was not simple disgust, not even the forced will of disgusted attention; there is a drive toward satiation, toward a complete absorption of the material in hand upon the outer film of the whole sensibility. . . . There is here that sentiment which is the posthumous and irresponsible achievement of shock; even sentimentality in reverse. Lawrence was rather vain of his achievements in this line."[4] It was a technique which could have led him farther in the direction to be taken by the early "black" satirists of the thirties, Céline, Miller, Durrell, and others who used the medium of "sick" or scatological horror. In the particularized grisliness of episodes in *Seven Pillars*—most notoriously in the hospital chapter (cxxi)—and in the excremental imagery of *The Mint*, Lawrence had perhaps contributed to fathering the genre. In the thirties one might have thought there were literary limits, or at least legal limits, to the extension of "blackness" in subject and language, to the extension of that sensuous participation forced upon the reader. A generation later Lawrence's experiments in revulsion seemed somewhat quaint and timid.

In love with speed, T.E. had written in his "Confession of Faith" poem, "in speed we hurl ourselves beyond the body." He always wanted to do a book on the subject. "I could write you pages on the lustfulness of moving swiftly,"[5] he confided to Robert Graves; and when Graves and Laura Riding (who had been doing printing and publishing via the Seizin Press) suggested his writing "a little book for us to print on the subject of Speed" he said that the idea appealed to him, that "speed, and especially the conquest of the air, was the greatest achievement of civilisation, and that it was one of the very few subjects now left to write about. All right, he would try." But on November 8, 1930, he wrote to Graves, "I am sorry about that book on Speed: but I cannot. The itch to write died in me many years ago, and I do not think it will revive. I hope not, for writing was a vexation and disappointment to me."[6] Yet he had written something on the subject earlier—

he claimed—in a letter to F. L. Lucas the year before. "Speed is a wonderful thing. I wrote a string of articles about [motor-] bike rides: but the *Motor Cycle* paper would not take them—so this is the sole survivor."[7] Apparently an essay was enclosed, but it has not come to light. If a journal *had* refused them—perhaps because T.E. insisted on pseudonymity —Lawrence went no further: the book he had discussed with Graves may have been aborted even before Graves and Lawrence had discussed the idea.

A further suggestion from Graves was that Lawrence provide himself with regular income from the book trade by going to "some big immoral publisher" and offering to permit his name to be put on its list of directors—a feature of most London firms' letterheads—for a fee of a thousand pounds a year. Graves even phrased the proposal, which concluded, "I shall be ready to advise you about books and to help you get promising authors, but I shall not bind myself to hours of work or office routine." Given T.E.'s active involvement in promoting promising young authors and his compulsive bent for criticism—both interests filled significant segments of his letters—it was a realistic idea. "They'd jump at it," Graves urged. "Even a small, not immoral publisher would accept. If you're too shy to do it I know how to do it for you without compromising either of us."[8] But Lawrence refused to consider it, although he continued to do—at no retainer—what Graves had suggested he do on a formal basis.

Another suggestion came from Mrs. Bernard Shaw—that T.E. write his autobiography. It failed to take hold, and the only sustained writing Lawrence produced after the *Odyssey* was a piece of purely technical writing—a pamphlet which was the product of his post-India service with R.A.F. seaplane-tender watercraft. A minor by-product of the experience was a self-consciously literary *Leaves in the Wind* fragment which described a seaplane crash to which Lawrence went to the rescue in a speedboat tender. Six airmen, "crushed together in the crushed canister of the hull," he noted, "were bubbling out their lives. Great belches of air spewed up." That incident apparently resulted in some additional Lawrentian technical writing, a report used by the board of inquiry in the case. "Now, did you notice the jury's rider on that Air Force crash?" Bernard Shaw afterwards asked Edwin Samuel. "Well, when I read that, I saw at once [that] it was 'Shaw.' No one else at Portsmouth* could write like that. 'Shaw' is in the bottom rank of the Air Force. The rank above requires a knowledge of reading and writing: but, whenever an exam [for promotion] comes along, 'Shaw' has become illiterate. Nevertheless, whenever a specially difficult order has to be issued, they always call in 'Shaw' to draft it."[9]

The 200 Class Royal Air Force Tender Seaplane pamphlet Lawrence produced at Plymouth was a technical manual with no literary pretensions—laconic, straightforward, exact— but it remains a model of its kind. His instructions for approaching a crashed aircraft or disabled boat in the tender, although not "literature" in its elevated sense, demonstrate his ability to be humane while providing relatively jargon-free technical advice:

Approaching a Moving Object, or Crash
223. The approach to any moving object will naturally be made following its direction, so that steerage way can be kept on the boat. The universal

---

* G.B.S. meant Plymouth.

rule is to drop speed a considerable way off the object, so as not to over-shoot or call upon the engines to stop the boat. Only just enough advantage in speed over the object should be kept for choosing the time to come along-side it. A fast approach, with a sharp opening of the engines in reverse, will cause the boat's own wash to over-ride her and throw her off or against the object, depriving her of control for the critical moment—which is danger-ous for the boat and uncomfortable for the passengers, besides looking and sounding clumsy.

. . . .

225. In safe circumstances never approach a crash or tow from the weather or tide side, as it will drift away; but circle it, and come up bow to wind or tide, or both, or the best compromise. Keep away, if time permits, to see if the object or the boat is the faster down tide or wind. If the object is faster, make it travel past the bows.

226. If there is danger of fire or explosion in a crash, approach only from the weather side. It may be desirable to come in stern-on, to keep the forward efficiency of the engines and rudder for sudden get-away. Care should be taken to post a lookout aft, in such a case to warn the coxswain of any wreckage that might endanger the boat to foul the propellers. The methyl-bromide fire extinguishers will extinguish any small quantity of burning petrol upon the water; but the danger of its re-lighting must be borne in mind.[10]

In March, 1932, the manual was stenciled and duplicated for the use of crews and mechanics employed on the new R.A.F. speedboat; Lawrence's last "book" was as unpre-tentious in format as his first was sumptuous. "I pride my-self," he wrote afterward [*Letters*, No. 480], "that every sen-tence in it is understandable to a fitter."

A minor piece of technical writing of this period remains, strangely, Lawrence's only deliberate attempt at fiction, al-though critics will continue to dispute such a label for it by pointing to the more imaginative parts of *Seven Pillars*. In 1931 Robert Graves and Laura Riding, under the joint pseud-onym of "Barbara Rich," were writing a "burlesque novel" for Cape, and needed a convincing description of a fantastic autogiro to be used by the hero. Graves appealed to Lawrence, who answered, frugally, that on the back of his letter were

notes for a Jules Verne aircraft of about 1980 A.D. Too long for your need: rather technical perhaps. Only a rag, of course. Your letter did not give the date of your hero. If he is to be alive tomorrow, then perhaps his aircraft is a bit too advanced for him. . . . This machine would have to be oxygenated at full speed and height, of course. The designer should be a Spanish lady, I think; the aircraft trade being by 2000 A.D. entirely in the hands of modistes. . . . If the skit is too Verne-y, then cut out the technical terms till the paragraphs run: and delete the antennae like cat's whiskers and the rotor propulsion.

On the back was T.E.'s description of his fictional aircraft:

For the benefit of air-minded readers a short account may here be given of this admirable little machine, which had been specially designed to His Highness's requirements by Senora——, the Madrid [modiste] to provide the ultimate degree of private comfort consistent with safety and speed.

All structural members were drop-forgings of cellular colloidal infrasteel, rubber-faced. The monocoque hull was proofed against sound and temperatures by panels of translucent three-ply crodex, between whose films were managed the ducts and condenser areas of the evaporative-cooling system for the eleven Jenny-Ruras picric-electric motors in the under-body.

Their power units were universally coupled by oil transmission and magnetic clutches alternatively to the lifting vanes (for hover or direct ascent) or to the propulsive rotor for horizontal travel. The vanes were geared into centrifugal governors which automatically varied their lifting angle according to load and air resistance.

In the rotor, the blade-pitch was adjustable at will, for speed and air density. The blades were set (with a clearance at maximum protrusion of .05m.) in the internal drum of a rotor-turbine of (tractor) Townend type, revolving about the nose of the fuselage which was paired for lead-in and baffled for internal turbulence. The slip-stream was deflected by scoops at the exit upwards against the bearing surfaces of the vanes, to increase lift in rare atmospheres or from salt water. A syphon-regulated ballast tank was fitted, to trim by the tail when taxying in rough water. The aircraft's landing springs were castored for ease of garaging and retractable for marine use. Landing speeds as low as 4 k.p.h. (downward) and 2 k.p.h. (forward) were attained. The maximum speed at 22,000 m. was—k.p.h.

All controls were of course directional operated, at will, and gyroscopically stabilised. Baehlen beam-antennae (of four-cycle frequency) were energised by the rotor-brushes. These were set to indicate by sound-signal to the pilot the presence of any body of more than atmospheric density within 300 metres. At 200 metres they began to induce deflection in the controls, and absolutely refused nearer approach than 18 metres until the motors were throttled back to landing speed. Antaeus indicators recorded height and earth-direction continuously and nitro-generators supplemented the power-units at great elevations.[11]

Lawrence clearly enjoyed what he had done and possibly, given the incentive, could have improved upon his overtechnical performance; however he no longer had the internal motivation for sustained creative writing. The following year, 1932, his paragraphs appeared, mildly altered, in "Barbara Rich's" novel *No Decency Left*. By that time he was involved in the more serious technical writing associated with his R.A.F. responsibilities.*

Lawrence's hunger to be recognized as a writer was reinforced late in 1932, just when he needed reassurance, for London newspaper stories that September were attributing the development of the new R.A.F. speedboats to him. The air force, embarrassed by anything suggesting such indiscipline as leadership from the lower ranks, preferred public

---

* Another technical piece—a lengthy one—has never been published: "Power Boat Hull Reconditioning," a survey of the overhaul of R.A.F. marine craft at the Bridlington station in 1934 and 1935. Seventy-nine pages long, the manuscript (in Lawrence's hand) is prefaced, "I arrived at Bridlington on Tuesday November 13, 1934. Information concerning work prior to this date has been derived from contractors."[12] The book, T.E. notes, was "closed on 23.2.35." It had to be. It was the week of his discharge from the air force.

silence about his activities and spirited him back from the base at Southampton, where the work was being done, to the quiet of Plymouth. Since Lawrence had finished his speed-boat handbook he took the transfer philosophically, but he was worried anew about being catapulted prematurely out of the service when, from London via the Shaws, came an invitation to join the newly formed Irish Academy of Letters.

The academy was Yeats's idea. With Shaw's assistance he had planned a body of twenty-five members who were not only Irish but had done writing of an Irish nature, and ten associates of Irish ancestry but who neither resided in Ireland nor based their work on Irish themes. In a letter to prospective academicians early in September, Yeats and Shaw described the organization as an authoritative instrument to represent and act for belles-lettres in Ireland, where official censorship still limited the vigor of literary activity, although the people themselves had "a deep respect for intellectual and poetic quality." The jointly signed invitation by the two Irish recipients of the Nobel Prize for literature concluded on a humble note: "In making this claim upon you we have no authority or mandate beyond the fact that the initiative has to be taken by somebody, and our age and the publicity which attaches to our names makes it easier for us than for younger writers."[13]

From France James Joyce declined, writing Yeats that he wished the academy success without him. "My case, however, being as it was and probably will be, I see no reason why my name should have arisen at all in connection with such an academy: and I feel quite clearly that I have no right whatsoever to nominate myself as a member of it."[14] Among others proposed as associate members, Eugene O'Neill and

T. E. Shaw (as the invitation read) both accepted; Yeats wrote T.E. with pleasure that he was "among my chief of men, being one of the few charming and gallant figures of our time, & as considerable in intellect."[15] A flattered T.E. found the letter when he returned from leave and answered with a disclaimer that as a writer he was only "a flash-in-the-pan" and an apology for the lack of Irishness in his work. "It's not my fault, wholly, if I am not more Irish: family, political, even money obstacles will hold me in England always. I wish it were not so."[16]

Toward the close of 1932 he began fulfilling his new dignity as an academician with the much-delayed publication of his *Odyssey* translation. A reprieve from early discharge and a return to speedboat duty thereafter further boosted his morale but failed to turn him from his concern about his future as a writer. "Writing," he confided to a friend he had known since 1911, "has been my inmost self all my life, and I can never put all my strength into anything else. Yet the same force, I know, put into action upon material things would move them, make me [again] famous and effective. The everlasting effort to write is like trying to fight a feather-bed."[17]

In 1933 Lawrence was stationed in Southampton and regularly went out into Southampton Water in one of his experimental boats. His home base was then Felixstowe, from which he was sent out on temporary duty to stations where marine craft work was underway. He was gaining weight and getting gray and was over forty, all of which made him brood about where he was heading. It led to a letter to Charlotte:

Southampton
9 XII 33

. . . Something happened to me last night, when I lay awake till 5. You know I have been moody or broody for years, wondering what I was at in the R.A.F., but unable to let go—well last night I suddenly understood that it was to write a book called "Confession of Faith," beginning in the cloaca at Covent Garden,* and embodying The Mint, and much that has happened to me before and since as regards the air. Not the conquest of the air, but our entry into the reserved element, "as Lords that are expected, yet with a silent joy in our arrival." It would include a word on Miranshah and Karachi, and the meaning of speed, on land and water and air. I see the plan of it. It will take long to do. Clouds Hill I think. In this next and last R.A.F. year I can collect feelings for it. The thread of the book will only come because it spins through my head: there cannot be any objective continuity—but I think I can make it whole enough to do. . . . I wonder if it will come off. The Purpose of my generation, that's really it. . . . Three years hence we'll know.[18]

It was Charlotte's rejected autobiography idea, reworked into a peculiarly Lawrentian frame of reference, but the book never materialized.

Another abortive literary project had a longer history. Like Field Marshal Lord Wavell, who compiled an anthology he published as *Other Men's Flowers*, Lawrence had designs for what remained a private anthology of other men's poetry. Since it was to reflect his own personal, idiosyncratic tastes, he called it *Minorities*; he sent a handwritten notebook-anthology with that title to Charlotte Shaw from India late in 1927, naturally deprecating his tastes and aims in a forwarding letter. For seven years, he told her, he had carried with

* The public lavatory on the southwest side, into which T.E. descended before going into the nearby R.A.F. recruiting station. See the first pages of Chapter III above.

him a copy of the *Oxford Book of English Verse*, but its contents did not fit his "whim." As a result he had taken to copying into a notebook "the minor poems I wanted," on a basis of personal rather than academic criteria: "Some are small poems of big men: others the better poems of small men. One necessary qualification was that they should be in a minor key: another that they should sing a bit. So you will find no sonnets here." Although he might have entertained thoughts of publishing his anthology one day, it remained in his lifetime something to mention or show to rare friends and a source of personal comfort. "You live always within reach of shelves," he told Mrs. Shaw, "and can keep so many poets on tap that you won't feel how necessary a friend is such a notebook as this. Its poems have each of them had a day with me. That little hackneyed Clough, for instance, about light coming up in the West* . . . I read that at Umtaiye, when the Deraa expedition was panicking and in misery: and it closely fitted my trust in Allenby, out of sight beyond the hills. There's all that sort of thing, for me, behind the simple words."[19]

The searching for literary equivalents to his experience had a long history, beginning in 1906 when Lawrence was eighteen and spending a summer among crusader castles in France. After seventeen descriptive borrowings in a single letter to his mother he apologized, "You really must excuse this battery of quotations, but I have got into the habit of quoting appropriate lines to myself, and this time I thought I would put them on record." The scene had impressed him,

---

* Lawrence's reference is to the last line of Arthur Hugh Clough's "Say Not the Struggle Nought Availeth" (1849).

and each of the lines adopted "might have been written to suit it."

Like much of Lawrence's slim *œuvre*, *Minorities* seemed to be in constant revision and augmentation. In Arabia his comrades sometimes saw him copying into a small red notebook from one of the three volumes he managed to keep with him throughout the war—the plays of Aristophanes in the original Greek, Malory's *Morte d' Arthur*, and the *Oxford Book of English Verse*. Lawrence's own copy of the *O.E.V.* survives, with annotations and dates showing when he cited particular works as having special personal significance. Despite his complaint that its contents failed to fit his whim, twenty-four poems from it appear in *Minorities*.

The notebook was finally filled, he wrote Charlotte Shaw, in 1927. Yet even then he could not face the fact that the task was completed. "The book had only three or four empty pages when I sailed from Southampton [for R.A.F. service in India] and these I filled with a [Humbert] Wolfe poem and a scrap of Blake. In the last year I have slowly copied [all the poems] into another book (with a few blank pages) which will last me for another seven years."

Each of the 112 poems in the extant notebook, copied down without titles or authors as if T.E. had adopted them privately as his own, apparently had a crucial and revealing association with something in Lawrence's life. As a private anthology the work provides evidence of Lawrence's wide reading and love for nineties verse as well as that of his friends and contemporaries. As a guide to the tormented mind of T. E. Lawrence, every poem possesses a curious fascination. Published finally in 1971, *Minorities*[20] is now grist for future biographers as well as an index to Lawrence's literary tastes and impulses. Even in recording his own states of mind he turned to poetry.

In what was perhaps the earliest postwar reference to the collection, a letter to Robert Graves dated September 24, 1922, shortly after T.E. had become—briefly—Aircraftman J. H. Ross, Lawrence inquired, "Did I ever show you my private anthology? *Minorities*, I called it. You are not in it yet, because you haven't done that special note which runs through it." Graves never saw the notebook, yet conjectured overdramatically but well that it was "an anthology of poems in which the shadow of defeat hung over an individual will in conflict with a more powerful force."[21] When he sent Lawrence a book of his new poems in 1923, T.E. quickly responded, "There's a Minority in it." There is. "A Forced Music" is about a royal minstrel who in response to repeated demands from the king and queen for "more," suddenly flings down "his twangling harp" and flees the court. Although T.E. clearly felt that he was honoring his friend by representing him in the exclusive anthology, a case can be made for the poem's parallel to Lawrence's past.

Most entries appear to be more than mere homage to his acquaintances among the Georgian poets. Dozens of selections reflect his sense of disillusionment with, and distaste for, his achievements as well as himself. Like Keats he is "half in love with easeful Death," and Laurence Housman's "to be quit of self is to be blest"* is as typical as W. E. Henley's

---

*It is striking that Lawrence also copied down this poem in its entirety on the back of a manuscript page of *Seven Pillars*, something he would hardly have done if it had not reflected his agony of spirit at the time of writing (verso, page 415 of the manuscript, Bodleian Library, Oxford). The existence of the poem also corroborates a confession T.E. had made to Charlotte Shaw in 1927: "It was my literary method, in making the ms now in the Bodleian, to take its destroyed

description of the poet as a tool on God's workshop floor, "worn to the butt, and banished/ His hand for evermore." Donne's expression of disgust with his own birth ("that sin where I begun") appears along with such poems which decry mercenary ambition as Swinburne's "Is this worth life . . . to win for wages?" and Charles Hamilton Sorley's "We do not run for prize . . . / But we run because we must." Other verses reflect his war-prisoner experience (James Elroy Flecker's "Beneath me lay my Body's Chain and all the Dragons born of Pain") and his predicament as a writer (Siegfried Sassoon's "You've got your limitations; let them sing"). Others evoke the "S.A." of his dedicatory poem to *Seven Pillars* (F. L. Lucas's "I love not you but what I dream you") and the impact of his experience with the East (Walter de la Mare's "He is crazy with the spell of far Arabia"). Yeats's "small cabin" at Innisfree where "I shall have some peace" recalls Lawrence's desire for, and contentment with, his Clouds Hill cottage, while in the penultimate poem T.E.— clearly in a different mood—copied out Blake's "I turn my back to the east . . ./ For light doth seize my brain / With frantic pain." Finally there is William Morris' "Christ keep the Hollow Land," a fitting—and Eliotesque—last word for one who saw in his generation hollow men in a hollow land.

That *Minorities* was meant for private perusal makes it little different from the rest of Lawrence's literary activity: the *Seven Pillars* and *The Mint* were also intended for special,

---

original, paragraph by paragraph, and to dwell on each till it contained some one sentence, or cadence, or word only, which gave me pleasure. One per paragraph was the ration: because if each sentence had been pleasurable the thing would have become a surfeit. ...Now in 90% of the cases this point which gave me pleasure was a quotation more or less disguised."

almost-private audiences. T.E.'s literary impulses, never motivated by the desire for book income or for further public acclaim, were fed from within rather than from without. His largest body of writing—his private correspondence—is thus logically integral with the rest. Some of his earlier letters, in fact, have close textual associations with both *Seven Pillars* and *The Mint*, and were not only the first working-out of material in the books but were actually retrieved to help in the writing. What remained for him to write in his last years were more letters, which he poured out without letup—perhaps the raw material of never-to-be-written books.

The thousand Lawrentian letters published in various places by the end of the first generation after his death (572 of them in the *Letters* and 270 in the *Home Letters of T. E. Lawrence and His Brothers*[22]) represent only a fraction of the total which survives in private hands and in library collections.* As with all correspondences, even literary ones, many of the letters which have survived deal with the trivialities, the courtesies, the basic business of existence. Yet many of Lawrence's are rich in personal incident, yearning, and confession; metaphysical speculation; literary criticism and literary self-criticism; the history, politics, and geography of his world. They burn with self-doubt, gleam with arrogance and egotism, turn bleak with introspection, reach remarkable intensities of controlled hysteria, wearily achieve

* Only one letter written in Arabic seems to have survived, dated "Ramadan 17, 1336—June 25, 1918," and written to King Hussein to warn him of the strength of Turkish positions at Ma'an, and to report on the activities of the northern Arab force under the command of his son Feisal. "I beg you, sir," Lawrence closed, "to burn this letter after reading it, because I am writing to you about matters which I should have disclosed to you orally." Like most such injunctions, it went unheeded, and the letter was published in part for the first time in the *Times* of London on June 30, 1967.

temporary inner peace. In sum, since he was as guilty of candor as he was of concealment, they are the autobiography Charlotte Shaw had vainly urged upon him, for they are more faithful to fact than are his own memoir-books and closer to life in their arising out of emotional immediacy. As Irving Howe has observed:

> They are not letters written systematically out of one impulse or idea, a rigid notion of what a letter should be. Some, like the early ones, are interesting because they show us a typically intelligent English youth of a time we find increasingly hard to remember or imagine. Some, like the few from the war years, are valuable simply as a glass, transparencies upon action.
>
> Some, like those to Lionel Curtis, form a grave impersonal confession, not an unburdening of secrets, but the statement of a man in agony and quest. Others hold one by a sudden power in expression, sudden breakthroughs to candor of speech. Whether they are "great letters," in the sense Keats's surely are, need not trouble us for a moment. They are the letters of a man who deserves to live in the imagination of his time.[23]

In his last letters, Lawrence—by then a civilian without even the aimless busyness of service discipline—wrote of the bewilderment he felt adjusting to his vast new resources of theoretically productive time. To Lady Astor he described himself as puttering about as if "there is something broken in the works . . . my will, I think." To Eric Kennington, who wondered what T.E. was doing all alone at Clouds Hill, he wrote: "Well, so do I, in truth. Days seem to dawn, suns to shine, evenings to follow, and then I sleep. What I have done, what I am doing, what I am going to do, puzzle me and bewilder me. Have you ever been a leaf and fallen from your tree in autumn and been really puzzled by it? That's the feeling." It did not last long. Eleven weeks out of uniform were all that were allotted to Lawrence, hardly long enough to redirect his destiny as a writer. On the thirteenth of May, 1935, he swerved his motorcycle to avoid two boys on bicycles coming toward him on a narrow road. But he was going too fast, and lost control. Six days later he died, never having regained consciousness.

Two months before, Lawrence had written a friend: "After I'm dead my heirs may do what they please with my books. As prose they are out-of-date already—pre-Joyce, in fact."[24] His heirs released a trade edition of the subscription *Seven Pillars* soon after his death; selections of his letters and occasional writings were published within the next few years. Two decades later even the by-then-dated *Mint* was removed from storage and in several segments proved to be more Joycean than Lawrence had self-deprecatingly described it. Except for the many hundreds of unpublished letters, almost all of Lawrence's extant writings intended for print had, within a generation, seen publication in some form. It was a relatively small body of work upon which to base a literary reputation which could survive both the detractors and the cultists.

As Aldous Huxley put it, Lawrence was in the end defeated as a writer because in his writing as in everything else he was "a man of the conscious will." For Huxley it all added up to an intense irony.

[Lawrence] *wanted* to write well, and he wrote about as well as a conscious will can make one write. But the consciously willed style always, it seems to me, stops short of the best, the genuinely good. It is always what the other Lawrence calls "would-be." A consciously willed style is necessarily artificial; but not all artificial styles are of the "would-be" variety. To some people it comes natural to write artificially; they are artificial with freshness and unction—like Milton, for example. . . . But with T. E. Lawrence I never feel any freshness or spontaneity. His descriptions of nature, have an aridity about them that contrasts most painfully, for me at least, with the descriptions of such unwilled stylists as Ruskin, or D. H. Lawrence or (to take another and much smaller writer who has described the Arabian scene) even Kinglake. T.E. makes me think of Alfieri—to some extent as a man, but more as a writer; for Alfieri willed to be a great tragic poet and came as near to being one as will can make anyone. . . . As a character I find Lawrence extremely interesting. . . . He was a Charles de Foucauld,* whose tragedy it was to be incapable of opening himself to that which lies beyond the will. . . . Hence, one divines, a really appalling unhappiness and sense of frustration. If one wants a demonstration of the basic *misère de l'homme*, one could hardly choose better than Lawrence; for he had everything that the human individual, as an individual, can possess—talent, courage, indomitable will, intelligence, everything, and though his gifts permitted him to do extraordinary, hardly credible things, they availed him nothing in relation to "enlightenment," "salvation," "liberation." Nothing burns in hell except self-will, says the author of the *Theologia Germanica*. Lawrence had a self-will of heroic, even of Titanic, proportions; and one has the impression that he lived for the most part in one of the more painful corners of the inferno. He is one of those great men for whom one feels intensely sorry, because he was nothing but a great man.[25]

"Nothing but a great man"—Lawrence lived in daily dread of just such an assessment. Like the crusader castles themselves, subject of his first book, his writing occupies a commanding position—but over a route less often traveled than overflown. What will survive, as license of language turns *The Mint* into a period piece and new translations of the *Odyssey* become annual nonevents, are those works which illuminate the unforgettable Lawrence personality: his letters and the *Seven Pillars*. Few epics are lived and fewer written. As authentic epic, despite its stridency and its posturing, the

---

* Charles Eugène Foucauld (1858–1916) was a French explorer and ascetic who explored Morocco, then forbidden to Christians, as a Jewish rabbi, afterwards writing of his travels in *Reconnaissance au Maroc* (1888). A visit to Palestine caused him to become a Trappist monk in 1890, but he left the order in 1890 to become a hermit there and later in France and Algeria. He was killed by tribesmen of the fanatical Muslim Senussi sect.

Seven Pillars of Wisdom passes almost beyond literary criticism, for in it life and art are fused.

Lawrence is the only major character astride his own pages, subject as well as object of the literary impulse that persisted when every other ambition he had for himself proved transitory or distasteful. Whatever the literary merits of his small output, it will be discussed—and sometimes even read—as long as men's imaginations are stirred by "Lawrence of Arabia."

CHAPTER VIII

The Apocrypha:
The Literary Impact
of "Lawrence of Arabia"

FOLK HISTORY tends to blend the popu-
lar and literary treatments of a personality with the actual,
and Lawrence helped speed the process, aiding (or goading)
writers into creating elements of his own myth as well as
participating in the manufacture himself. Often this was done
by emphasizing a particular side of him: the quiet archeologist from Oxford; the white-garbed, jeweled-daggered
knight on a camel, seen in Lowell Thomas' book; the military
genius of Liddell Hart's biography; the shy, ubiquitous
former colonel, Private Meek, of Bernard Shaw's play *Too
True to Be Good*; the tortured, introspective leader of men de-
picted in his own *Seven Pillars*; the ascetic, masochistic recruit of his service chronicle. He permitted no film to be
made from *Seven Pillars* during his lifetime, however, telling
Sir Alexander Korda—who placed G.B.S.'s "Private Meek"
(Walter Hudd) under option for the purpose—to wait until
his subject was dead. Only a year later T.E. hurtled to his
death, but Korda made no film.

The legend kept growing as new Lawrences kept emerging
—the pathological liar and exhibitionist of Richard Aldington's "biographical enquiry" of 1954; the archetype of the
horror-haunted, twentieth-century intellectual of the 1955[1]
biography by the French historian Jean Beraud Villars; and
the physically and spiritually broken recluse of Terence Rattigan's *Ross*. Robert Bolt's literate, dramatic film script based
upon *Seven Pillars* offered yet another diagnosis of the riddle
of Lawrence's character.

Rattigan's *Ross*,[2] which managed successfully to blend
Seven Pillars of Wisdom into a frame-play based on *The Mint*,*
is built about the scaffolding of the last twenty-four hours of
Lawrence's five-month career as Aircraftman Ross. The cur-
tain rises on an R.A.F. depot near London in the winter of
1922. A businesslike flight lieutenant is dealing out summary
sentences to recruits guilty of minor infractions. Ross, a small
man, older than most recruits, is marched in and admits to the
charge of having been eighteen minutes late in returning to
camp on expiration of his pass. Interrogation reveals that he
has been in a motorcycle accident and had to run the rest of
the way to camp, having been left "with very little bicycle."
Pressing on with the inquiry, the lieutenant learns that Ross
had been away to "have a meal with some friends" at "a
place in Buckinghamshire." The recruit hesitates stubbornly
when asked his friends' names, but when the officer makes it
clear that the request is in order, Ross sighs out the names of

---

* Arnold Wesker's R.A.F. basic-training play *Chips with Everything* (1962) is
based on the playwright's own conscript experience but has so many close parallels to *The Mint* that Wesker must have also seen *Ross* or gleaned a good deal
from *The Mint* itself. (Wesker told an interviewer, however, that he had not
read *The Mint*.) For an analysis of the parallels see Stanley Weintraub, "Wesker's *Mint*," *London Review*, I (Winter, 1966), 27–34. The Wesker disclaimer
followed publication of this article.

Lord and Lady Astor, Mr. and Mrs. George Bernard Shaw, and the Archbishop of Canterbury. Enraged by what he considers a provocative answer, the lieutenant throws his pencil down, screams something about insubordination, and orders Ross marched out./

After Ross returns to his hut, a demobilized former officer —for economic reasons now in the ranks—identifies him as "Lawrence of Arabia," and attempts to blackmail him; but Ross, not rising with his billfold to the threat that the story will be sold to the press, pleads hopelessly to be allowed to find the peace he has sought as a private soldier. The play soon fades into flashback as Ross sleeps: troubled dreams shape themselves about Lawrence's rise to wartime leadership in Arabia and postwar notoriety as a lecture-circuit subject. Inherent in these glimpses into Ross's Lawrence-past is Rattigan's suggestion as to why the masks of "Ross" and later "Shaw" had to be adopted and the episode of "Lawrence of Arabia" closed ("I sicken myself").

The final scenes take place the next morning in the lieutenant's office. The story has broken; headlines in London papers bring the harassed commanding officer in to arrange for the immediate, and quiet, discharge of A/c 2 Ross. Naively, the lieutenant wonders aloud whether all the fuss and secrecy have anything to do with the insubordination charge he has scheduled for hearing. The commanding officer is incredulous: "You know who you've charged with insubordination? Lawrence of Arabia." "He was late on pass," the lieutenant protests, still not awake to the situation. "I asked him who he'd been with, that night. He said the Archbishop of Canterbury (*his voice begins to falter*), Lord and Lady Astor, and Mr. and Mrs. George Bernard—oh my God!"

Ross, in his last scene, is packing his kitbag. His barracks mates, unaware of his identity, uncomprehendingly look on, assuming that the discharge was ordered because the authorities thought that the quiet, older man did not "fit in." An airman asks him what he intends to do, and Ross quickly answers, "I'm going to get back into the R.A.F. as soon as I can." "Think you can do that?" "Well, I'll have to change my name, I suppose. Ross won't do anymore. Shaw. I thought of that this morning."

So goes the new legend of Lawrence's discharge as "Ross" and reincarnation as "Shaw," the name he was to keep the rest of his life. It is not history, but it is, unquestionably, the dramatic portrait of the playwright's subtitle: effective theater rather than chronology or literal fact. Like most writers of memorable plays based upon actuality, Rattigan has worried more about the illusion of history than about historicity, believing that the invented episodes that open and close this play are psychologically sound and might well have happened.[3]

The summary punishment scene and the under-wraps discharge scene the following morning are Rattigan's telescoping of history. They might well have happened—but did not. Time is again telescoped in the events of T.E.'s discharge. A month actually elapsed between the newspaper headlines (December 27, 1922) of "Lawrence of Arabia" in the ranks "seeking peace" and the quiet carrying-out of a cabinet-level discharge order on January 23, 1923. Other facts, too, are altered for dramatic effectiveness, a technique of which T.E. himself was a master. Lawrence claimed that an officer had recognized him (no attempt at blackmail was ever mentioned) and sold the information to a newspaper for thirty pounds—a suspiciously Judas-like number. Rattigan changes the officer to a former officer serving in the ranks—an improvement upon Lawrence's history—and raises the price to one hundred pounds. Also, the sympathetic barracks companions of Ross, through the last scene, give no indication that they recognize Ross to be any more than a recruit unemployable in civilian life and too old to have the stamina to begin again in the ranks. Their ignorance adds irony as well as compassion to the close. Lawrence himself realized that his presence was an open secret and that his hut companions often sheltered him from unwanted attention.

Another episode in *Ross* interprets, rather than alters, history. The flashback into Lawrence's Arabian adventure is treated with highly dramatic ambiguity in *Seven Pillars*. Rattigan indulges in some dramatic speculation, based upon Lawrence's writings about the episode, that when T.E. was whipped and abused at Deraa his will was broken by the traumatic awakening he experienced: that he had recognized himself as a latent homosexual. Further, Rattigan deduces, the Turkish commander ordered the torture of Lawrence not primarily because he fancied his prisoner himself and was refused, but rather to break the will of the self-styled Circassian whom Rattigan deduces the Turk knew all the time was really his disguised enemy, Lawrence. In the Rattigan version, the general tells Lawrence, who is half-conscious, face down on the floor:

You can hear me, I think. . . . You must understand that I know. . . . I do pity you, you know. You won't ever believe it, but it's true. I know what was revealed to you tonight, and I know what its revelation will have done to you. You can think I mean just a broken will, if you like. That might have destroyed you by itself. But I mean more than that. Far more. (*An-*

grily.) But why did you leave yourself so vulnerable? What's the use of learning if it doesn't teach you to know yourself as you really are? . . . For you, killing wasn't enough. (*He lifts Lawrence's head again*.) You had to be —destroyed. . . . The door at the bottom of the stairs through there is unlocked. It leads into the street.

The play's theory—a very appealing one—is that all of Lawrence's life thereafter constituted a series of attempts on his part to achieve personal triumphs of the will—a will the Turks assumed had been destroyed. It assumes, however, that the Turkish general knew who Lawrence was, feared him as an enemy, but believed that the best way to destroy the Arab revolt would be not to kill its inciting force but to return him to the Arabs broken in body and spirit. Deprived not of Lawrence's physical presence, but of his charismatic value as a rallying and unifying factor, the Arabs would find T.E.'s usefulness inverted. However, would a general indulge in the hazard of returning the enemy's field commander when he could do away with him?

The theatrical potential in *Seven Pillars* alone has been demonstrated in the film *Lawrence of Arabia*, a visually outstanding motion picture released in 1962–1963 and successfully reissued since. Cinema's contribution to the enigma, although it dramatizes the essentials of Lawrence's Arabian experience, is yet another source of future folk-history about Lawrence. For example, in *Seven Pillars of Wisdom*, near the successful end of the march to Damascus, Lawrence writes of encountering, in the village of Tafas, Turkish atrocities of such ghastliness that in revulsion at the sight he gave orders to exact revenge if the guilty enemy units could be overtaken. "By my order," he writes in Chapter cxvii, "we took no prisoners, for the only time in our war." Lawrence never forgave himself, although at that point no order of his could have stopped the enraged, vengeance-seeking Arabs. From the Tafas episode the Robert Bolt film script builds a portrait of a Lawrence driven by (although ashamed of) blood-lust.

Regularly Lawrence tried—and sometimes failed—to check the Arab killing of captured Turks, an impossibly difficult task. To the Arabs, after centuries of tribal rivalries, plunder and murder of the enemy were basic to warfare. British officers who accompanied Lawrence testified later to his efforts to prevent wanton killing both in, and on the way to, Damascus. Wherever it was possible—in desert country often devoid of food and water and shelter—Lawrence insisted that his men take prisoners as well as booty. But he chronicles also that "the Turks did not take Arab prisoners. Indeed, they used to kill them horribly; so, in mercy, we were finishing those of our badly wounded who would have to be left helpless on abandoned ground."

Possibly Bolt, turning from *A Man for All Seasons* to his homework for the film script of *Lawrence of Arabia*, came upon Jean Beraud Villars' biography. Villars suggests dramatically that T.E.'s wartime activities "filled him with horror as did the sudden flashes of cruelty which he often felt rising in him. He realized with fear that he had within him the stuff and tastes of a killer"; he paradoxically follows this with a tale from *Seven Pillars* which describes Lawrence, reconnoitering alone far in advance of his lines, coming upon a Turkish soldier asleep. Awakened, the Turk gazed in panic at the pistol which T.E. held in his hand and then looked desperately at his own rifle, which lay where he had left it, now out of reach. Lawrence said to him quietly, "God is merciful," and continued his survey.

The film "establishes" Lawrence's pathological sadism early, through his confession to General Allenby at their first meeting that he once led an Arab servant to his death in quicksand and executed another Arab with a pistol, and "didn't like" his discovery that he had actually "enjoyed it." According to *Seven Pillars*, however, the servant boy Daud died of exposure at Azrak, when Lawrence was far away to the south. Daud's companion Farraj is later mortally wounded, and (acting on prearranged agreement among themselves) rather than let him fall into Turkish hands—the Turks were then burning alive the hapless wounded they encountered—Lawrence kills him. "I knelt down beside him," Lawrence recalled, "holding my pistol near the ground, by his head, so that he should not see my purpose; but he must have guessed it, for he opened his eyes and clutched me with his harsh, scaly hand. . . . I waited a moment and he said 'Daud will be angry with you,' the old smile coming back so strangely to his grey shrinking face. I replied 'Salute him from me.' He returned the formal answer 'God will give you peace,' and at last wearily closed his eyes."

Nevertheless, neither Farraj nor Daud is "Gasim"—who is executed by Lawrence in the film. This is apparently Gasim el Shimt, whom Lawrence does rescue from abandonment in the desert and who is only referred to briefly afterwards. The "Gasim" of the film is telescoped with Hamed the Moor, who earlier (xxi) had wantonly murdered Salem, of the Ageyl tribe, while they were on a journey with Lawrence. The Ageyl cried out for vengeance and, with a blood feud between the Ageyl and his Moroccans in the offing, Lawrence—his head aching with fever—"desperately" suggested a formal execution: "I told Hamed [in the film he does not know at first that the villain is the man he saved] that he must die for punishment, and laid the burden of his killing on myself. Perhaps they would count me not qualified for feud. At least no revenge could lie against my followers; for I was a stranger and kinless." The account of the killing—which, to his horror, Lawrence first bungled—follows. The task leaves his night sleepless, and, sick with fever and horror, he has to be lifted into his camel's saddle as they depart the area in predawn darkness. Only the fact that Lawrence describes everything—the majestic and the sordid—with graphic brilliance provides any excuse for the screen interpretation, since it can be argued that what one lingers over in horror is what—at least subconsciously—is actually appealing.

The film, due to the reticence necessary in 1962, skimps another vital episode—the one upon which Rattigan based *Ross*. But Lawrence's capture, torture, and apparent homosexual humiliation by the Turks were then considered to be dubious material for widescreen color. Nevertheless, the incident was far more significant in terms of the motivation for T.E.'s later behavior than can be understood from a suggestive pinch and a beating, followed by a toss into the street. Equally skimped—for less understandable reasons—is any picture of the real General Allenby, the only other major English figure not disguised in the film. Allenby becomes the stage English general, discussing confidential military strategy at the top of his voice in the officer's mess and talking to Lawrence as much about poetry and growing roses as about battle plans.

Emir Feisal, about whom Lawrence vainly centered his hopes for Arab unity, is an equally romantic figure. In reality a lover of Arab bards and Turkish gossip, in Bolt's invention he becomes the heir of the Arab intellectual zenith, musing to Lawrence that the medieval Arab city of Cordova had two miles of publicly lit streets at a time when London was still a village. His English guest adds, "And the Caliphs studied Plato when the Kings of England couldn't write." Yes, sighs Feisal with romantic despair, the Moslems *were* a great nation nine centuries ago. Mildly (according to the screen directions) the film Lawrence suggests, "Time to be great again, my lord." The conversation is part of a manufactured episode early in the film which telescopes and romanticizes the scenes in *Seven Pillars* in which Lawrence visits the Arab chiefs as an inexperienced young lieutenant and comes away convinced of the military value of a general Arab uprising against the Turks.

In a final, ironic distortion, the screen Lawrence becomes an unwitting traitor, not to the British, but to the Arab cause, for—stupified (supposedly) with wanton slaughter that leaves his white Bedouin robes red, his arms bloody to the elbows, and his face twisted with fiendish joy—he allows Allenby and the British army to march into Damascus while the orgy goes on nearby, losing the chance to seize, unaided, the symbol of an Arab Arabia. The implication that earlier occupation of Damascus would have thwarted an Anglo-French division of Middle Eastern spoils agreed to years earlier is, at best, naive. The suggestion that Allenby and his troops cynically took advantage of Lawrence's alleged indulgences in sadism to reach Damascus first is false: an Anzac patrol entered the city fifty minutes before Lawrence's men, but this had no effect upon the situation, nor was it a result of the Deraa massacre. The portrait of Lawrence gleefully up to his elbows in gore is not "the madness born of the horror of

Tafas" about which Lawrence has written, and the supposed emotional irresponsibility which sells out the Arabs at the moment before triumph is good film melodrama but not good history. Nevertheless, we see or read plays about historical personages not because they recount history or formulate historical theory accurately or well, but because they tell us intriguing stories about interesting people. T.E. (as Ross or Shaw—or Lawrence) was one of those perennially fascinating persons whose every move—or motive—made (and still makes) a good story.

Even in his own time Lawrence fed the literary impulses of novelists and playwrights. It was inescapable that he would turn up as a character in fiction; he did so—in the 1920s alone—in novels ranging from John Buchan's *Courts of the Morning* and Maurice Barrès' *Un Jardin sur l'oronte* (see Chapter 1 above) to D. H. Lawrence's *Lady Chatterley's Lover*, in which Mellors, the gamekeeper who had been an officer in India, is described by Connie Chatterley as "like Colonel C. E. Florence, who preferred to become a private soldier again." But her confidant "had no sympathy with the unsatisfactory mysticism of the famous C. E. Florence. He saw too much advertisement behind all the humility. It looked [like] just the sort of conceit the knight most loathed, the conceit of self-abasement." Later André Malraux, who had written sensitively about T.E. as man and writer, put Lawrence into *The Walnut Trees of Altenburg* (1952), where Vincent Berger "could perhaps have found some means of destroying the mythical person he was growing into, had he been compelled. But he had no wish to do so. His reputation was flattering. What was more important, he enjoyed it." Also, what Berger likes about war is "the masculine companionship, the irrevocable commitments that courage imposes." James Aldridge followed with *Heroes of the Empty View* (1954), in which "Gordon or Gordion" is an Arab desert leader who wears Bedouin robes but is "Scotch or Welsh or even Irish" and right out of the *Seven Pillars*. And Anthony West attempted to sustain his readers' sense of history in his novel *David Rees Among Others* (1970) via a lengthy, malicious, and gratuitous chapter dominated by a character identified as T. E. Lawrence. But the most interesting nondramatic works inspired by Lawrence and his writings were by poets of the 1930s, although even earlier T.E. had fought shoulder to shoulder with W. B. Yeats's fantasy alter ego, Michael Robartes. ("Young Colonel Lawrence never suspected the nationality of the old Arab fighting at his side.")

C. Day Lewis, whom Lawrence had encouraged as a poet, put Lawrence into a mystery novel he wrote under his *nom de plume* of Nicholas Blake. *Shell of Death* (1936), an early work by the future poet laureate, overliterary and full of improbabilities, utilizes the Lawrence of the postretirement months in 1935, disguised by pallor and a beard—almost as if D. H. Lawrence had been grafted onto T. E. Lawrence. Still the identity of the Irishman whose origins are shrouded in mystery is never in doubt. "Great Scott!" exclaims private eye Nigel Strangeways. "*The* Fergus O'Brien? The legendary airman. The Mystery Man who Retired from Life of Dare-Devil Adventure to Seclusion of English Countryside." O'Brien is a now-retired R.A.F. veteran who led a charmed life in and out of the war, keeping his "grip on the popular imagination" by being "something out of the ordinary run of 'heroes.' " He risks his life in air crashes, takes a native fort in Afghanistan single-handed, and flouts military authority regularly, even wearing irregular uniform (complete with carpet slippers). As Sir John explains, "Authority has always been a red rag to him—he didn't give a damn for orders. Went too far, finally. After the war, when his flight was out East, he was ordered to bomb some native village. He didn't see why the natives should have their village blown to pieces just because some of them hadn't paid their taxes, so he made his flight loose off their bombs in the middle of a desert and then flew low over the village, dropping 1-lb. boxes of chocolates. . . . He was politely asked to resign."*

After his retirement O'Brien attempts to fend off the press but is a victim of newspaper "Mystery Man publicity" and under an assumed name lives in a starkly furnished army hut (rather than the "Dower House") on a large estate, among books inscribed to him by the authors, including, prominently, a fine *Arabia Deserta*. "He told me," one character confides, "a lot of Munchausen sort of stories about his adventures in the war and after; at least if anyone else had told them they would have been pure Munchausen, but I had heard enough about him to know that they were probably true. Founded on fact, anyway—you know how an Irishman will garnish a true story with any number of picturesque falsehoods just to make it more appetising. Fergus was a true artist in that."

Although W. H. Auden years afterwards cited his *The*

* The episode suggests an escapade of Aubrey Bagot, the less obvious of the two Lawrence figures in Shaw's *Too True to Be Good*, which Day Lewis probably knew. While Private Napoleon Alexander Trotsky Meek contentedly runs the army from his place in the ranks, Aubrey Bagot, also a former flying officer and gentleman, determines to violate all his former instincts out of guilt for the wartime killing of helpless civilians; and he becomes a burglar and confidence man.

Orators (1932) as an example of "the fair notion fatally injured"—a reference to its obscurity—one of its clearest elements is its indebtedness to T. E. Lawrence, who crops up
often in Auden's writings of the early 1930s. Part of the first
book of the poem concerns the search for a hero, a redeemer,
a savior. In its second book, "Journal of an Airman," appears
such a hero, who has in him (besides Auden's then-obligatory
Marxist elements) something of Aircraftman Shaw. His
sense of guilt and isolation are extreme, and there is a suggestion of homosexuality as well as of permanent adolescence.
On the positive side he preaches man's commitment to the
new element, air, overthrowing his bonds of land and water.
Here the point is probably politically symbolic, but it is
literally close to Lawrence's public views during his R.A.F.
years.

Auden also wrote about Lawrence in the Cape house publication *Now and Then* in the spring of 1934, two years after
The Orators, quoting with reference to T.E.'s life-style a passage from Lenin, who had written that one must "go hungry,
work illegally and be anonymous. . . . The self must learn to
be indifferent." In 1933, a year after *The Orators*, Auden further represented Lawrence in "A Happy New Year" as an
airman passing negative judgment upon England and Englishmen, flying over the country and dropping a derisive note to
that effect. In *The Ascent of F6*, the play he wrote with Christopher Isherwood in 1936, he again based his hero, Ransom,
partly on Lawrence. "Like Shelley and like Baudelaire,"
Isherwood noted separately at the time, "it may be said of
him that he suffered, in his own person, the neurotic ills of an
entire generation."[4] That was "why my friends and I found
him so fascinating," he wrote a generation later. "He was the

myth-hero of the 'thirties. Auden and I consciously tried to recreate him in our character of Michael Ransom in *F6.*"[5]

In the Auden-Isherwood play Ransom is the hero of exceptional courage and tenacity, driven by the "deep cleavage" in his own nature to undertake impossible quests. As another member of the Auden group, Louis MacNeice, put it, the poet, "being so interested in the phenomenon of the man of action (for example, in Colonel Lawrence), many of his lyrics contain in condensed form what is worked out at length in the play, *F6*—the tragedy of the man who gets his own way."

As man and writer—and the two were always inescapably intertwined—Lawrence invited adaptation into the work of other writers. The hero as uneasy adventurer, the hero with the guilty conscience, the hero as man of mysterious origins, the hero testing himself to the uttermost limits, the hero leading the independence movement of an alien race, the hero as introspective intellectual or as deliberately declassed aristocrat: all these and more had been the stuff of legend and story from the times of the scops, bards, and minstrels. That they existed in a single, real, twentieth-century man provided a curious literary impulse for Lawrence's contemporaries. Yet if he had not existed, writers would have had to invent him.

Notes

NOTES TO CHAPTER I

1. Leonard Woolley and T. E. Lawrence, *The Wilderness of Zin* (London, 1915) quoted in David Garnett (ed.), *The Essential T. E. Lawrence* (New York, 1951), 62.

2. Winston Churchill confirms the episode in *Great Contemporaries* (London, 1937), 156, and Horace Rumbold, in Philip Knightley and Colin Simpson, *The Secret Lives of Lawrence of Arabia* (New York, 1970), 156, quotes the king as having been surprised by Lawrence's "bad language" in refusing the decoration.

3. This information was taken from a single manuscript sheet, "History of Seven Pillars," written by Lawrence in 1927 and now in the Humanities Research Center, University of Texas, Austin.

4. "The Politics of Mecca," as quoted from the document in the Foreign Office archives in Knightley and Simpson, *The Secret Lives of Lawrence of Arabia*, 52–53.

5. "The Conquest of Syria," *ibid.*, 58–59.

6. "Twenty-Seven Articles" (extracts from Articles 18–19, 20, and 27), *ibid.*, 63–64.

7. This account and Lawrence's other early postwar publications that anticipated *Seven Pillars* or were developed from stages of the larger work as it evolved were published as Stanley and Rodelle Weintraub (eds.), *Evolution of a Revolt: Early Postwar Writings of T. E. Lawrence* (University Park, Pa., and London, 1968).

8. Lawrence's wartime *Arab Bulletin* contributions were collected posthu-

mously as T. E. Lawrence, *Secret Despatches from Arabia* (London, 1939), a limited edition of one thousand copies, with a preface by A. W. Lawrence.

9. Robert Graves to Rodelle and Stanley Weintraub, March 22, 1968.

10. The 96-page manuscript, including the unpublished Parts I, V, VI, and VII, is in the collection of the Humanities Research Center, University of Texas, Austin.

NOTES TO CHAPTER II

1. Hugh Walpole, Introduction to the Limited Editions Club edition of George Borrow, *Lavengro* (London, 1936), vi.

2. Denis de Rougemont, "Prototype T.E.L.," trans. Richard Howard, *Dramatic Personages* (New York, 1964), 139.

3. George Bernard Shaw, autograph notes in Charlotte Shaw's copy of *Seven Pillars of Wisdom*, Arents Collection, New York Public Library.

4. David Garnett (ed.), *The Letters of T. E. Lawrence* (London and New York, 1938), No. 257.

5. *Ibid.*, No. 327.

6. S. N. Behrman, *Portrait of Max* (New York, 1960), 279.

7. Robert Payne, "On the Prose of T. E. Lawrence," *Prose*, No. 4 (Spring, 1972), 104.

8. T. E. Lawrence to E. M. Forster, September 29, 1924, in Garnett (ed.), *Letters*, No. 255.

9. James Notopoulos, "The Tragic and the Epic in T. E. Lawrence," *Yale Review*, LIV (1964–65), 333–34.

10. V. S. Pritchett, *Books in General* (London, 1953), 38.

11. Richard Aldington, *Lawrence of Arabia* (London, 1955), 328–29.

12. Clifton Fadiman, "T. E. Lawrence," *New Yorker*, September 28, 1935, p. 67.

13. R. A. Scott-James, *Fifty Years of English Literature* (New York, 1951), 19–92.

14. Sulieman Mousa, *T. E. Lawrence: An Arab View* (New York, 1966), 98.

15. Winston Churchill, *Great Contemporaries*, (London, 1937), 133–34.

16. Jean Beraud Villars, *T. E. Lawrence, or, The Search for the Absolute*, trans. Peter Dawnay (London, 1958), 296–97.

17. Jan Kott, *Shakespeare Our Contemporary* (London, 1964), 94.

18. Fawn Brodie, *The Devil Drives: A Life of Sir Richard Burton* (New York, 1967), 105.

19. Herbert Read, *A Coat of Many Colours* (London, 1945), 26, 24, 26.

20. Malcolm Muggeridge, "Poor Lawrence," *New Statesman*, LXII (October 27, 1961), 604.

21. E. M. Forster, *Abinger Harvest* (New York, 1936), 146.

22. Andrè Malraux, "Lawrence and the Demon of the Absolute," *Hudson Review*, VIII (Winter, 1956), 525.

23. *Ibid.*, 532.

24. Quoted in Guy Chapman's introduction to the reissue of his *A Passionate Prodigality* (New York, 1966), unpaged.

NOTES TO CHAPTER III

1. T. E. Lawrence, *The Mint* (London, 1955; New York, 1935, 1955).

2. T. E. Lawrence to Charlotte Shaw, January 4, 1928, in Add. Ms. 45903, 4 (British Museum); Stanley Weintraub, *Private Shaw and Public Shaw: A Dual Portrait of Lawrence of Arabia and G.B.S.* (New York, 1963), 144.

3. Lawrence, *The Mint*, 13–14.

4. See George Bernard Shaw to T. E. Lawrence, April 12, 1928, in Weintraub, *Private Shaw and Public Shaw*, 149.

5. Weintraub, *Private Shaw and Public Shaw*, 150.

6. Lawrence to Shaw, May 9, 1928, in David Garnett (ed.), *The Letters of T. E. Lawrence* (London and New York, 1938), No. 357.

7. Lawrence to E. M. Forster, August 6, 1928, in Garnett (ed.), *Letters*, No. 364; Lawrence to Forster, July 5, 1928, in A. W. Lawrence (ed.), *Letters to T. E. Lawrence* (London, 1962), 66–68.

8. Lawrence to David Garnett, June 14, 1928, in A. W. Lawrence (ed.), *Letters to T. E. Lawrence*, No. 360.

9. Siegfried Sassoon to Lawrence, November 13, 1930, in A. W. Lawrence (ed.), *Letters to T. E. Lawrence*, 156–57.

10. Sholto Douglas, *Years of Command* (London, 1966), 144–45.

11. Philip Knightley and Colin Simpson, *The Secret Lives of Lawrence of Arabia* (New York, 1970), 264.

12. Lawrence to Jonathan Cape, quoted in Michael S. Howard, "The Reluctant Money-Spinner," London *Times Saturday Review*, January 9, 1971, p. 15.

13. Wyndham Lewis to Frederick Morgan, May 6, 1955, in W. K. Rose (ed.), *The Letters of Wyndham Lewis* (London, 1963), 561.

14. R. P. Blackmur, "The Everlasting Effort: A Citation of T. E. Lawrence," in *The Lion and the Honeycomb* (New York, 1955), 111–12.

15. The drawing is reproduced in Weintraub, *Private Shaw and Public Shaw*, 33.

16. George Bernard Shaw to Stephen Winsten, in Stephen Winsten, *Days with Bernard Shaw* (New York, 1949), 267.

NOTES TO CHAPTER IV

1. Jean Beraud Villars, *T. E. Lawrence, or, The Search for the Absolute*, trans. Peter Dawnay (London, 1958), 271.

2. T. E. Lawrence to Bruce Rogers, January, 1931, in David Garnett (ed.), *The Letters of T. E. Lawrence* (London, 1938), No. 431.

3. C. M. Bowra, "Two Translations," *New Statesman and Nation*, April 8, 1933, p. 449.

4. Ronald Storrs, *Orientations* (London, 1937), 524.

5. Kimon Friar, "Attic Rime of the Ancient Mariner," *Saturday Review*, July 8, 1961, pp. 20-21.

6. *Ibid.*, 21.

7. "On Translating Homer," *Times Literary Supplement*, March 14, 1968, p. 242.

8. David Garnett to Lawrence, December 21, 1932, in A. W. Lawrence (ed.), *Letters to T. E. Lawrence* (London, 1962), 86.

9. *The Odyssey of Homer: Newly Translated into English Prose*, trans. T. E. Shaw (New York, 1932), Book v.

10. Erich Lessing, *The Adventures of Ulysses: Homer's Epic in Pictures* (New York, 1970). The entire text is Lawrence's translation.

11. Lawrence to H. G. Andrews, March 6, 1935, quoted in the Charles Hamilton auction catalog, viii, May 20, 1965, p. 27.

12. James Notopoulos, "The Tragic and the Epic in T. E. Lawrence," *Yale Review*, LIV (1964–65), 331–45.

NOTES TO CHAPTER V

1. Robert Graves, *On Poetry: Collected Talks and Essays* (New York, 1969), 579.

2. T. E. Lawrence to C. J. Greenwood, July 21, 1931, in a private collection.

3. Lawrence to E. M. Forster, April 23, 1928, in David Garnett (ed.), *The Letters to T. E. Lawrence* (London and New York, 1938), No. 352.

4. F. L. Lucas to Stanley Weintraub, June 20, 1965, in the possession of the authors.

5. C. Day Lewis, *The Buried Day* (London, 1960), 216.

6. *Ibid.*, 222.

7. Lawrence to Jonathan Cape, November 14, 1923, in Garnett (ed.), *Letters*, No. 230.

8. T. E. Lawrence, *T. E. Lawrence to His Biographers Robert Graves and Liddell Hart* (2 vols.; New York, 1963), I, 142–43.

9. Lawrence to Charles Doughty, July 30, 1920, in Garnett (ed.), *Letters*, No. 128.

10. Lawrence to David Garnett, November 30, 1927, in *Fifty Letters: 1920–1935. An Exhibition* (Austin, Tex., 1962), 24–25.

11. Lawrence to Ronald Storrs, February 25, 1935, in Ronald Storrs, *Orientations* (London, 1937), 527.

12. Lawrence to Francis Yeats-Brown, quoted in A. W. Lawrence (ed.), *T. E. Lawrence by His Friends* (London, 1937), 423–24.

13. *Spectator*, August 6, 1927, p. 223.

14. *Ibid.*

15. *Ibid.*

16. *Spectator*, September 10, 1927, pp. 390–91.

17. *Ibid.*, February 25, 1928, pp. 368–69.

18. H. G. Wells to Yeats-Brown, quoted in A. W. Lawrence (ed.), *T. E. Lawrence by His Friends*, 424.

19. T. E. Lawrence to Robert Graves, December 24, 1927, in Lawrence, *To His Biographers*, I, 144.

20. T. E. Lawrence, "The Works of Walter Savage Landor," in David Garnett (ed.), *The Essential T. E. Lawrence* (New York, 1951) 288–90.

21. *Ibid.*

NOTES TO CHAPTER VI

1. Cape described this side of T. E. in A. W. Lawrence (ed.), *T. E. Lawrence by His Friends* (London, 1937), 466–75; Michael Howard's biography, *Jonathan Cape, Publisher* (London, 1971), adds further details also utilized in this chapter.

2. The inscription, dated February 23, 1929, is quoted in *Fifty Letters: 1920–1935. An Exhibition* (Austin, Tex., 1962), 28.

3. T. E. Lawrence to Edward Garnett, October 4, 1923, in David Garnett (ed.), *The Letters of T. E. Lawrence* (London and New York, 1938), No. 222.

4. Quoted in Philip Knightley and Colin Simpson, *The Secret Lives of Lawrence of Arabia* (New York, 1970), 184.

5. *Ibid.*, 184–86.

6. Quoted in J. M. Wilson (ed.), *Minorities*, preface by C. Day Lewis (New York, 1972), 29.

7. Quoted in Knightley and Simpson, *The Secret Lives of Lawrence of Arabia*, 180.

8. Edward Marsh, *A Number of People: A Book of Reminiscences* (London, 1938), 344.

9. See David Garnett (ed.), *The Essential T. E. Lawrence* (London, 1951), 291, where the poem is printed in full.

10. *Ibid.*

11. Charlotte Shaw to "T. E. Shaw," March 14, 1927, in Janet Dunbar, *Mrs. G.B.S.: A Portrait* (New York, 1963), 249.

NOTES TO CHAPTER VII

1. T. E. Lawrence to Philip Sassoon, March 30, 1933, in David Garnett (ed.), *The Letters of T. E. Lawrence* (London and New York, 1938), No. 486.

2. These pages appear in Garnett (ed.), *Letters*, as Nos. 292, 338, 433, and a bracketed, unnumbered entry between Nos. 559 and 560.

3. Garnett (ed.), *Letters*, No. 292. (This is not a letter, however, but a fragment labeled "Leaves in the Wind.")

4. R. P. Blackmur, "The Everlasting Effort: A Citation of T. E. Lawrence," in *The Lion and the Honeycomb* (New York, 1955), 117.

5. T. E. Lawrence to Robert Graves, November 8, 1930, in T. E. Lawrence, *T. E. Lawrence to His Biographers Robert Graves and Liddell Hart* (2 vols.; New York, 1963), 166.

6. *Ibid.*

7. T. E. Lawrence to F. L. Lucas, March 26, 1929, in Garnett (ed.), *Letters*, No. 376.

8. Robert Graves to T. E. Lawrence, Autumn, 1933, in A. W. Lawrence (ed.), *Letters to T. E. Lawrence* (London, 1962), 109.

9. Edwin Samuel, *A Lifetime in Jerusalem* (New York, 1970), 113–14.

10. Quoted in David Garnett (ed.), *The Essential T. E. Lawrence* (London, 1951), 308–309, which contains additional extracts from the manual.

11. Barbara Rich [pseud.], *No Decency Left* (London, 1932), 153–55. Lawrence's original, from which the quotation is taken, is reprinted in T. E. Lawrence, *To His Biographers*, I, 168–69.

12. The manuscript is in the Humanities Research Center, University of Texas, Austin.

13. Allan Wade (ed.), *The Letters of W. B. Yeats* (London, 1954), 801–802.

14. James Joyce to W. B. Yeats, October 5, 1932, in Stuart Gilbert (ed.), *Letters of James Joyce* (New York, 1957), 325.

15. W. B. Yeats to T. E. Lawrence, September 26, 1932, in A. W. Lawrence (ed.), *Letters to T. E. Lawrence*, 213.

16. T. E. Lawrence to Yeats, October 12, 1932, in Garnett (ed.), *Letters*, No. 464.

17. T. E. Lawrence to Ernest Altounyan, January 9, 1933, in Garnett (ed.), *Letters*, No. 479.

18. T. E. Lawrence to Charlotte Shaw, December 9, 1933, in Add. Ms. 45903, 4 (British Museum).

19. *Ibid.*, quoted by Philip Knightley and Colin Simpson, *The Secret Lives of Lawrence of Arabia* (New York, 1970), 297–98.

20. J. M. Wilson (ed.), *Minorities*, preface by C. Day Lewis (New York, 1972).

21. T. E. Lawrence to Robert Graves, September 24, 1922, in T. E. Lawrence, *To His Biographers*, I, 21.

22. M. R. Lawrence (ed.), *Home Letters of T. E. Lawrence and His Brothers* (London, 1954).

23. Irving Howe, "T. E. Lawrence: The Problem of Heroism," *Hudson Review*, xv (1962–63), 364.

24. T. E. Lawrence to H. G. Andrews, March 6, 1935, in T. E. Lawrence, *To His Biographers*, I, 142–43.

25. Aldous Huxley to Victoria Ocampo, December 12, 1946, in Grover Smith (ed.), *Letters of Aldous Huxley* (New York, 1969), 559.

NOTES TO CHAPTER VIII

1. Jean Beraud Villars, *T. E. Lawrence, or, The Search for the Absolute*, trans. Peter Dawnay (London, 1958). The book was published in its original French in 1955.

2. Terence Rattigan, *Ross: A Dramatic Portrait* (London, 1960). *Ross* was first produced on May 12, 1960, at the Haymarket Theatre, London.

3. Terence Rattigan to Stanley Weintraub, October 7, 1960, in the possession of the authors.

4. Christopher Isherwood, review of A. W. Lawrence (ed.), *T. E. Lawrence by His Friends*, in the *Listener*, 1937; reprinted in Christopher Isherwood, *Exhumations* (New York, 1966), 24.

5. Isherwood, *Exhumations*, 13.

Selected Bibliography

WORKS BY T. E. LAWRENCE

The Advance of the Egyptian Expeditionary Force Under the Command of General Sir Edmund H. H. Allenby, July 1917 to October 1918. Compiled from Official Sources and Published by the Palestine News. Edited by C. H. C. Pirie-Gordon. Cairo: Government Press, 1919. Two text sections are from reports by Lawrence: "Sherifian Cooperation in September" and "Story of the Arab Movement."

Crusader Castles. 2 vols. London: The Golden Cockerel Press, 1936. T.E.'s undergraduate thesis, augmented with additional material.

Evolution of a Revolt: Early Postwar Writings of T. E. Lawrence. Edited by Stanley and Rodelle Weintraub. University Park, Pa., and London: The Pennsylvania State University Press, 1968. Includes Lawrence's newspaper and periodical journalism, from articles in the London *Times* of November, 1918, to extracts from a version of *Seven Pillars* in *The World's Work* in 1922.

Fifty Letters: 1920–1935. An Exhibition. Austin, Tex.: Humanities Research Center, 1962. Catalog of the exhibition, illustrated with reproductions of many of the letters.

The Forest Giant, by Adrien le Corbeau. Translated from the French by J. H. Ross [T. E. Lawrence]. London: Jonathan Cape, 1924; New York: Harper & Brothers, 1924.

The Home Letters of T. E. Lawrence and His Brothers. Edited by M. R. Lawrence. Oxford: Basil Blackwell, 1954.

Introduction to *Travels in Arabia Deserta*, by Charles M. Doughty. Boston and London: The Medici Society and Jonathan Cape, 1921.

Introduction to *The Twilight of the Gods and Other Tales*, by Richard Garnett. London: John Lane [1924]; New York: Dodd, Mead and Company, [1924].

Letters of T. E. Lawrence. Edited by David Garnett. London: Jonathan Cape, 1938; New York: Doubleday, 1938.

Men in Print: Essays in Literary Criticism. Introduction by A. W. Lawrence. London: Golden Cockerel Press, 1940. Includes a facsimile reproduction of a manuscript essay and Lawrence's identified *Spectator* contributions of 1927–28.

The Mint. Notes Made in the R.A.F. Depot between August and December, 1922, and at Cadet College in 1925 by 352087 A/C Ross. Regrouped and Recopied in 1927 and 1928 at Aircraft Depot, Karachi. New York: Doubleday, Doran, and Company, 1936; London: Jonathan Cape, 1955.

Minorities. Edited by J. M. Wilson, with a preface by C. Day Lewis. London: Jonathan Cape, 1971; New York: Doubleday, 1972. T.E.'s personal anthology of verse.

The Odyssey of Homer: Newly Translated into English Prose. Translator's Note by T. E. Shaw [T. E. Lawrence]. New York: Oxford University Press, 1932.

Oriental Assembly. Edited by A. W. Lawrence. London: Williams and Norgate, Ltd., 1939. Includes the first printing of the suppressed first chapter of *Seven Pillars*, now incorporated into all editions.

Revolt in the Desert. New York: George H. Doran Company, 1927; London: Jonathan Cape, 1927. Abridgment of *Seven Pillars*.

Secret Despatches from Arabia Published by Permission of the Foreign Office. Preface by A. W. Lawrence. London: Golden Cockerel Press, 1939. Lawrence's *Arab Bulletin* contributions.

Seven Pillars of Wisdom: A Triumph. Subscription Edition. London: Privately printed, 1926; Trade editions. London: Jonathan Cape, 1935, and New York: Doubleday, Doran and Company, 1935.

T. E. Lawrence to His Biographers Robert Graves and Liddell Hart. 2 vols. London: Faber, 1938; New York: Doubleday, 1963.

Two Arab Folk Tales. London: Corvinus Press, 1937. "Taken from the beginning of the diary which T.E.S. kept while travelling in Northern Arabia during 1911."

The Wilderness of Zin. [With Leonard Woolley.] London: Palestine Exploration Fund, 1915; Jonathan Cape, 1936.

WORKS ABOUT T. E. LAWRENCE

The T. E. Lawrence literature is immense, and during his lifetime as well as after his death it threatened to become a major publishing industry. Little of it, however, has dealt with the man as writer. This checklist identifies mainly those works primarily concerned with Lawrence as a man of letters and a few additional books and articles of inescapable significance to the Lawrence life and legend.

BIBLIOGRAPHY

Clements, Frank A. *T. E. Lawrence: A Reader's Guide.* Hamden, Conn.: Shoe String Press, 1973.

Disbury, David G. *T. E. Lawrence of Arabia: A Collector's Booklist.* Privately printed, 1972.

Duval, Elizabeth. *T. E. Lawrence: A Bibliography.* New York: Arrow Editions, 1938.

Meyers, Jeffrey. *T. E. Lawrence: A Bibliography.* New York: Garland Publishing Inc., 1975. Essentially a separate printing of the bibliography to Meyers' *The Wounded Spirit*, cited below. The updated bibliography lists about 900 entries by and about T.E.L.

CRITICISM

Aldington, Richard. *Lawrence of Arabia: A Biographical Enquiry.* London: Collins, 1955. Reprint edition with introduction by Christopher Sykes, 1969.

Al-Said, Nuri. Introduction to the Arabic edition of *Revolt in the Desert*, *Near East*, xxxi (April 28, 1927), 496–97.

Armitage, Flora. *The Desert and the Stars: A Portrait of T. E. Lawrence*. London: Faber, 1956.

Blackmur, R. P. "The Everlasting Effort: A Citation of T. E. Lawrence." In his *The Lion and the Honeycomb*. New York: 1955. Pp. 97–123. This article was originally published in 1940.

Bowden, Ann. "The T. E. Lawrence Collection at the University of Texas." *Texas Quarterly*, v (Autumn, 1962), 54–63.

Churchill, Winston. "Lawrence of Arabia." In his *Great Contemporaries*. London: Butterworth, 1937.

Edmonds, Charles [Carrington, Charles Edmund]. *T. E. Lawrence*. London: Davies, 1935.

Forster, E. M. "T. E. Lawrence." In his *Abinger Harvest*. New York: Harcourt, Brace, 1936.

Fox, Ralph. "Lawrence the Twentieth Century Hero." *Left Review*, No. 10 (June, 1935), 391–96.

Garnett, David, ed. *The Essential T. E. Lawrence*. London: Penguin, 1951; New York: Dutton, 1951. Includes extracts from Lawrence's "Leaves in the Wind" and *200 Class Seaplane Tender*.

Graves, Robert. *Lawrence and the Arabs*. London: Cape, 1928.

Henighan. "T. E. Lawrence's *Seven Pillars of Wisdom*: Vision as Pattern." *Dalhousie Review*, li (Spring, 1971), 49–59.

Howard, Michael S. *Jonathan Cape, Publisher*. London: Cape, 1971. The T.E.L. material is usefully extracted in "The Reluctant Money-Spinner," the *Times* (London) *Saturday Review*, January 9, 1971, p. 15.

Howe, Irving. "T. E. Lawrence: The Problem of Heroism." *Hudson Review*, xv (1962–63), 333–64.

Hull, Keith N. "T. E. Lawrence's Perilous Parodies." *Texas Quarterly*, xv (Summer, 1972), 56–61.

Kiernan, Reginald Hugh. *Lawrence of Arabia*. London: Harrap, 1935, 1947.

Knightley, Philip, and Colin Simpson. *The Secret Lives of Lawrence of Arabia*. London: Nelson, 1969; New York: McGraw-Hill, 1970. Expansion of their 1968 *Sunday Times* articles.

Lawrence, A. W., ed. *Letters to T. E. Lawrence*. London: Jonathan Cape, 1962.

————, ed. *T. E. Lawrence by His Friends*. London: Jonathan Cape, 1937. Includes as an appendix a listing of the books in T.E.'s Clouds Hill library, with transcriptions of flyleaf inscriptions where they appear.

Lewis, Wyndham. "Perspectives on Lawrence." *Hudson Review*, VIII (Winter, 1956), 596–608.

Liddell Hart, B. H. *"T. E. Lawrence": In Arabia and After*. London: Jonathan Cape, 1934.

MacPhail, Andrew. *Three Persons*. London: John Murray, 1929.

Malraux, André. "Lawrence and the Demon of the Absolute." *Hudson Review*, VIII (Winter, 1956), 519–32; *World Review*, II (August, October, 1949), 9–12, 33–37.

————. *The Walnut Trees of Altenburg*. London: John Lehmann, 1952.

Marsh, Edward. *A Number of People: A Book of Reminiscences*. London: William Heinemann, 1938. The essay on Lawrence also appeared in *Harper's*, CLXXIX (July, 1939), 173–74.

Maugham, Robin. *Nomad*. New York: Viking Press, 1948.

Meyers, Jeffrey. "E. M. Forster and T. E. Lawrence: A Friendship." *South Atlantic Quarterly*, LXIX (Spring, 1970), 205–16.

————. "Nietzsche and T. E. Lawrence." *Midway*, XI (Summer, 1970), 77–85.

————. "The Revisions of *Seven Pillars of Wisdom*." *PMLA*, LXXXVIII (1973), 1,066–82.

————. *The Wounded Spirit: A Study of Seven Pillars of Wisdom*. London: Martin Brian & O'Keeffe, 1973.

Mills, Gordon. "T. E. Lawrence as a Writer." *Texas Quarterly*, X (Autumn, 1962), 35–45.

Muggeridge, Malcolm. "Poor Lawrence." *New Statesman*, LXII (October 27, 1961), 604.

Mousa, Sulieman. *T. E. Lawrence: An Arab View*. London and New York: Oxford University Press, 1966.

Notopoulous, James A. "The Tragic and the Epic in T. E. Lawrence." *Yale Review*, LIV (1964–65), 331–45.

Nutting, Anthony. *Lawrence of Arabia: The Man and the Motive*. London: Hollis and Carter, 1961; New York: Clarkson Potter, 1961.

Ocampo, Victoria. *338171, T.E.* (*Lawrence of Arabia*). Translated by David Garnett. New York: Dutton, 1963; London: Gollancz, 1963. The Spanish original was first published in 1942.

Payne, Robert, "On the Prose of T. E. Lawrence." *Prose*, No. 4 (Spring 1972), 91–108.

———. *Lawrence of Arabia*. New York: Pyramid Books, 1962.

Pritchett, V. S. "Ross at the Depot." *New Statesman*, XLIX (February 19, 1955), 251.

———. "T. E. Lawrence." In his *Books in General*. London: Chatto & Windus, 1953.

Rattigan, Terence. *Ross: A Dramatic Portrait*. London: Hamish Hamilton, 1960.

Read, Herbert. *A Coat of Many Colours*. London: 1945. G. Routledge, "Lawrence of Arabia," pp. 19–23, and "The Seven Pillars of Wisdom," pp. 24–26.

Richards, Vyvyan. *T. E. Lawrence*. London: Duckworth, 1939.

Rota, Bertram. "Lawrence of Arabia & *Seven Pillars of Wisdom*." *Texas Quarterly*, v (Autumn, 1962), 46–53.

Rougemont, Denis de. *Dramatic Personages*. New York: Holt, Rinehart and Winston, 1964. "Prototype T.E.L.," translated by Richard Howard, pp. 135–51. The French original was published in 1947.

Sprigg, Christopher St. John [Christopher Caudwell]. "T. E. Lawrence: A Study in Heroism." In his *Studies in a Dying Culture*. London: Lawrence and Wishart, 1938. Pp. 20–43.

Thomas, Lowell. *With Lawrence in Arabia*. London: Hutchinson, 1924; New York: Garden City, 1924. New enlarged edition. New York: Doubleday, 1967.

Toynbee, Arnold. *Acquaintances*. New York and London: Oxford University Press, "Colonel T. E. Lawrence," pp. 178–97.

Villars, Jean Beraud. *T. E. Lawrence, or, The Search for the Absolute*. Translated by Peter Dawnay. London: Sidgwick and Jackson, 1958. The French original was published in 1955.

Warner, Oliver. "Scott, Lawrence and the Myth of British Decadence." *National Review*, CLXXVII (September, 1941), 314–17.

Weintraub, Stanley. *Private Shaw and Public Shaw: A Dual Portrait of Lawrence of Arabia and G.B.S.* New York: Braziller, 1963; London: Jonathan Cape, 1963.

Weintraub, Stanley and Rodelle. "Chapman's Homer." *Classical World*, LXVII (September–October, 1973), 16–24.

————"*Moby-Dick* and *Seven Pillars of Wisdom.*" *Studies in American Fiction*, III (Fall, 1974), 238–40.

Woodhouse, C. M. "T. E. Lawrence: New Legends for Old." *Twentieth Century*, CLVII (March, 1955), 228–36.

Index